422

Tax Deductions

For Businesses
& Self Employed Individuals

by Bernard B. Kamoroff, C.P.A.

Laytonville & Willits, California

Published by
BELL SPRINGS PUBLISHING
Box 1240, Willits, California 95490
telephone 707/459-6372   fax 707/459-8614
e-mail: info@bellsprings.com
www.bellsprings.com

Third Edition (Revised), 7th Printing
Updated as of January, 2002
Library of Congress Catalog Number 00-108531
ISBN: 0-917510-19-4

Design, color and page layout: Thanks to Sharon Kamoroff.
Cover layout thanks to Jeanne Koelle
Cartoons and photographs used with permission of copyright holders:
IRS Help Line cartoon, courtesy Bill Webster.
Sister Ruby cartoon, courtesy John Grimes.
Professional Writer cartoon, courtesy Mort Gerberg.
Don't You Dare Deduct Me cartoon, courtesy William Hamilton.
IRS Files and Office photographs, courtesy Internal Revenue Service.
Sacramento Tax Files photo by Dan Chan, courtesy Franchise Tax Board.
Most People Bring Their Accountant cartoon, courtesy Boardroom Reports.

Quantity Purchases:
We offer substantial discounts on bulk sales to organizations,
schools, professionals, and businesses. For more information,
call (707) 459-6372.

Please Read:

I have done my very best to give you useful and accurate information in this book, but I cannot guarantee that the information is correct or will be appropriate to your particular situation. Laws and regulations change frequently and are subject to differing interpretations. It is your responsibility to verify all information and all laws discussed in this book before relying on them. Nothing in this book can substitute for legal advice and cannot be considered as making it unnecessary to obtain such advice. Obtain specific information from the Internal Revenue Service or a competent person.

You Can Keep This Book Up To Date:

This edition of **422 Tax Deductions** is current as of the date shown on the copyright page. Every January, we publish a one-page **"422 Tax Deductions Update"**, listing changes in tax laws, referenced to the corresponding entries in the book. If you would like a copy of the Update, send a self-addressed, stamped #10 envelope (business size) and $1.00 to: **422 Update, Box 1240, Willits, CA 95490.**

Special Thanks To...

Ace tax accountant Larry Jacobs of Oakland, California.
Thanks also to Jan Zobel and Tom Walz for tax help.
Thanks to Leigh Robinson for the English lesson.
Thanks to my wife Sharon Kamoroff for cover, color and page layout ideas, and for all around support.

The only thing that hurts more than having to pay income tax is not having to pay income tax.
                                                                    —*Thomas R. Duwar*

A Treasure Hunt

Every business owner is looking for ways to reduce expenses without cutting corners, without reducing quality, or losing customers. But few businesses look to the one area almost guaranteed to save you money: your tax return.

Last year, America's small businesses overpaid their income taxes by over two billion dollars, according to a C.P.A. study reported in *Business 2000* Magazine. The overpayments were made because the businesses failed to take tax deductions they were legally entitled to take. Many of these businesses are still unaware of their errors. They overpaid their taxes and don't even know it.

The IRS is not going to help these businesses. The IRS will never tell you about a tax deduction you didn't claim. That's up to you.

Whether you struggle with your own tax return, hire an accountant, or put your trust in a software program, the more you know about what's deductible, the more you'll save on your taxes. Your tax return lists only a handful of deductions, so it is up to you to make sure you find and claim every one. It really is a treasure hunt.

Every tax deduction you find in this book will reduce your taxes, honestly, legitimately, and with the full approval and blessings of the Internal Revenue Service.

It is very much like finding free money.

Contents

If the adjustments required by section 481(a) and Regulation 1.481-1 are attributable to a change in method of accounting initiated by the taxpayer, the amount of such adjustments, to the extent such amount does not exceed the net amount which would have been required if the change had been made in the first taxable year, shall be taken into account by the taxpayer in computing taxable income in the manner provided in section 481 (b) (4) (B) and paragraph (b) of this section.
—Internal Revenue Code

Well as through this world I've rambled
I've seen lots of funny men.
Some will rob you with a six-gun
And some with a fountain pen.
—Woody Guthrie, "Pretty Boy Floyd"

Relax

Relax. Tax law isn't easy, but this book is.

This book will not try to explain how to prepare a tax return. This book will not have you struggling with tax forms. This book will not drag you through the confusing, contradictory, confounding world of tax law.

This book *will* let you know about hundreds of tax deductions that are available to every small business, every home business, every self-employed individual, every independent contractor, full-time or part-time.

A CPA by the name of George Brown, who was interviewed in a business magazine, made a statement that has stuck with me for several years and that inspired this book: "You get a raise every time you can legitimately avoid paying a tax on something." Every tax deduction you find will save you money on your federal income taxes, on your state income taxes, on your self employment taxes, on local income taxes, and on any other business taxes based on net profit.

If you really like the challenge of preparing your own tax return, I encourage you to do it. And if you don't want to struggle with tax forms, leave that miserable job to your tax accountant. Either way, you owe it to yourself to find every tax deduction you can.

Who Is This Book For?

This book is for anyone working for himself or herself. This includes sole proprietors, partners in partnerships, members of limited liability companies (LLCs), and people who own their own corporations.

This book is for shopkeepers, repair people, manufacturers, trades people, freelancers, professionals, independent contractors, outside contractors, subcontractors, general contractors, entrepreneurs, consultants, artists, craftspeople, direct marketers, network marketers, multi-level marketers, free agents, sales reps, inventors, employers, moonlighters, home businesses, full-time, part-time, sideline, you name it. Unless you are on someone else's payroll as an employee, you are in business for yourself. You are entitled to all the business deductions in this book.

This book is for anyone running a business on the Internet. All deductions related to the Internet are included.

This book is also for anyone who gets a 1099-MISC form, the IRS's "Miscellaneous Income" form that businesses must give to individuals who are doing contract work but are not on the payroll as an employee.

This book is *not* for employees: people on the payroll of an employer, having taxes deducted from their paychecks, getting a W-2 statement at year end. (If you are an employee/owner of your own corporation, this book *is* for you).

This book is *not* for investors, people making money in the stock market or commodities trading, people earning their money from rental income or loans or interest or dividends, people earning what the IRS calls "passive" income. This book is for people who invest in their own businesses, but not for people who invest in other people's businesses.

How to Use This Book to Your Best Advantage

Be forewarned. This guide does not provide complete information on all federal tax laws nor was it intended to. There are already enough publications available that do just that, and they are not easy to read either.

This guide does list every business tax deduction I have encountered in twenty years of tax practice, consulting, writing, teaching, and running my own businesses. I let you know what the deductions are, and whether they apply to you and your business.

Tax laws are precise, and I've tried to make this book as precise as possible, but without making it so confusing and complicated that it becomes unreadable—like most of the tax guides on the market. I've tried to accomplish this task with a three step system:

Step One: For each tax deduction, I define the terminology (and *not* in IRS Code Sections, accountant's jargon, or other forms of Advanced Sanskrit), and I explain the basic laws. These laws apply to most businesses, most of the time. "Most" is the key word. There may be exceptions.

Step Two: If there are exceptions to the laws, or complications, or special situations for some businesses, I alert you to these fun details and explain them in general, but without bogging you down in confusing or complicated tax law.

Step Three: If necessary, I refer you to one of the free IRS publications that have the fine-print details of the laws. You can then do your own research (which really isn't all that difficult if you take it one deduction at a time), or you can ask your accountant about the details. Either way, you now know that there may be yet another tax savings worth looking into.

Also understand that the wording in tax law is important. The words have very specific meanings. Don't read more into the laws than what is explained here, don't read between the lines, don't make assumptions, as you can easily wind up making assumptions that are inaccurate.

If the terminology is confusing or unclear, if you do not understand a word, a definition, or an explanation, it is important that you stop, and take the time to understand its meaning before using the information. If you don't fully understand the concepts, ask. Get help from your accountant. Misunderstanding tax law can lead to trouble.

I'd also like to give you a warning about getting help from the IRS. Although IRS publications are usually accurate and reliable, the same cannot always be said of tax information the IRS gives out over the phone or in person. The IRS people do, on occasion, give out totally incorrect information. Tax laws are vastly complicated and even the experts make mistakes. Do not rely on verbal information unless you can verify it. Ask the IRS person for a reference in one of their publications, and look it up.

Expense Category

Every deduction listed in this book includes an expense category. The expense category is a guide to help you fill out your tax return, to figure out what line on the tax return to post each deduction.

Schedule C, the business tax return for sole proprietors, lists only 22 categories of expense: 22 line items. The partnership tax return (Form 1065), the Limited Liability Company tax return (also using Form 1065), the C corporation tax return (Form 1120), and the S corporation tax return (1120-S) list a similar number of categories. And here we have 422 deductions to combine into 22 categories. Where do the 422 deductions go? What categories?

Some categories are obvious. Interest goes on the "Interest" line. Advertising goes on the "Advertising" line. Pencils go on the "Office expense" line. But where do you stick Education expenses? Freight? Decorating expenses? Alarm systems? You can use the "Expense category" designations in the book as a guide.

Keep in mind that these expense categories are only a guide. They are not law, not rigid. It is not critical which deductions go on which lines on the tax form. The IRS is not going to be upset if an expense that belongs on one line winds up on another. Even I'm not sure whether some deductions should be labeled "Office expense" or "Supplies" or something else. If you have a deduction you don't know where to put on the tax return, just pick a reasonable category and put it there.

It is a good idea to make a worksheet showing which expenses you combined for the tax return, and keep it with your copy of your return (no need to send it to the IRS). This will make things a lot easier should you ever face an audit, or if you need to check your figures later, or if you are just looking back a year later trying to figure out how to fill out the next year's tax return.

There is a line on the tax return called "Other expenses," used for deductions that don't fit into any other category. Many of the deductions in this book are shown as "Other expenses," because I could not find an appropriate category on the tax return. But remember that the category you pick is not critical. What is critical is that you take every deduction you are entitled to, regardless of where you put it on the tax return.

Deductions you do include as part of "Other expenses" must be listed individually. The tax return provides a separate area for listing the deductions that comprise "Other expenses." List each expense separately, then show the total on the "Other expenses" line on the return.

Is Every Possible Tax Deduction Listed?

This list of 422 deductions is compiled from my studies of tax laws for over twenty years (somebody's got to do it, right?), my background as a C.P.A., my experience working directly with hundreds of different businesses of all types, and the generous feedback I've gotten from my readers and people who attend my seminars.

But still, I'd be a fool to say that I've listed every possible deduction there is. If you have a deduction not listed in this book, and if it meets the basic rules for all deductions (covered below), by all means take it. Or at least ask your accountant about it. And let me know about it too, will you? Maybe the next edition of this book will be called "423 Tax Deductions."

Isn't This What You Pay Your Accountant For?

Here is the most important piece of information in this book: You have to find these deductions yourself. Only you know the ins and outs of your own business. You cannot rely 100% on your bookkeeper, your accountant, your attorney, your software program, or the Internal Revenue Service.

Any experienced tax accountant will (or certainly should) know about every tax deduction listed in this book. But your accountant can't possibly take the time to ask you—and his or her 300 other tax clients—about every possible deduction you didn't know about or failed to include on your ledgers. The typical tax accountant may have several hundred tax clients, and during the three hectic months of "tax season" (January 15 to April 15), your accountant is preparing a dozen or maybe two dozen tax returns a day. The accountant most likely wants to take your year's totals, totals you yourself have summarized from your ledgers, enter them into the computer, push "Print," and collect his $250. Next.

If you are expecting an accountant to actually sit down with you, discuss tax deductions in detail, study your business and your ledgers, and find you savings, you should plan to do this well before the tax preparation time, and expect to pay about $100 an hour for this service. And even then, you really should not expect an accountant who does not work day to day in your business to be able to rattle off every possible tax deduction you may be entitled to.

Instead, spend a few hours with this book. Skim the alphabetical list of deductions, and spot the ones that may apply to you. And then, if needed, ask your accountant about them. Your accountant will be of much greater help, and much greater value, if you first go through these 422 deductions before seeing the accountant. By doing a little homework, you may significantly reduce the accounting fees.

The well known tax attorney Julian Block said it best: "The informed client gets the best advice."

Will Your Deductions Trigger An Audit?

Are you afraid to take certain deductions because you fear they may trigger an audit? Welcome to the club. There are thousands of small business people paying millions of dollars in taxes they don't owe, year after year, simply out of fear of being audited.

"Don't take the home office deduction, it'll guarantee an audit." What home business owner hasn't heard that? It is a myth. The home office deduction does not invite an audit. And the same applies to most tax deductions.

But, yes, there are a few tax deductions that are Red Flags, ones likely to bounce your return out of the computer, to put that nasty gleam in the eye of some IRS auditor, deductions that are likely to invite an audit, and, again yes, ones you may want to avoid—or at least be very careful about—when preparing your tax return.

Those few deductions that are likely to invite an audit are mentioned in this book. They include: Large travel and entertainment deductions, probably the most likely to generate suspicion. Deductions for expenses not typically associated with your type of business. Deductions for items of a personal or recreational nature. Any large deductions out of line with the amount of income you are reporting. (Although a home office deduction does not trigger an audit, a *large* home office deduction combined with a small income does increase your chances of being audited).

What *will* increase your odds of being audited are not so much the deductions, but other things on your tax return: A loss year after year. An occupation targeted by the IRS because of potential "abuse" (ease of cheating), particularly businesses that deal in cash (laundromats, cab drivers). Barter transactions. Major changes from year to year (you say you are a lawyer one year and a psychiatrist the next). Non-business items that are incorrect or out of line. Claiming your dog as a dependent. Telling the IRS that the income tax is unconstitutional.

If you discover from reading this book that you have a tax deduction that may cause you trouble, it is then up to you to decide how "aggressive" you want to be, or how safe you want to be, when claiming the tax deduction. I think this book will help you make those decisions. But I recommend you talk to your tax accountant about your concerns. Any good accountant should be able to help you stay within your comfort zone.

I think that is the real key: your comfort. No amount of money is worth destroying your peace of mind. No tax savings is worth high blood pressure. But short of a sleepless night of IRS worries, if you are entitled to a tax deduction, take it. The laws were written to allow these deductions. Congress and the IRS say, "Yes, take the deductions, you don't owe the tax." If the government in its wisdom is allowing a deduction, you in your wisdom should take it.

When in Doubt, Deduct

Even after all the studying, talking to experts, and getting deep into the Internal Revenue Code, sometimes you still cannot be positive that a certain deduction is or isn't legitimate. The Internal Revenue Service says one thing, the Tax Court says the exact opposite, and your Congressman (who dreamed up the law) is still on vacation. What do you do?

The answer depends on your own personality, how comfortable or uncomfortable you are if you have to face an audit, and of course how much is at stake. If you are only going to save a few bucks but might get a Dear Taxpayer letter from the IRS (and maybe open up a Pandora's box you'd rather stay closed) it's probably not worth the risk.

But if you have nothing to hide and lots to save, I personally would go for it. Your chance of being audited, no matter what you deduct, is less than 5%. If you do get audited, the worst that can happen is the IRS will say No Dice, and demand the back taxes you'd owe anyway, and interest. There is usually no penalty for making an honest mistake or a reasonable interpretation of the law.

I want to make one thing clear throughout this book: If any deduction is questionable, if there is any doubt, any disagreement, any IRS opposition, I spell that out very clearly in the description of the deduction. You will not be caught by surprise, you will not have to wonder if a certain deduction can lead to possible trouble.

Tax Loopholes

I also want to make it clear that this book is not about "tax loop-holes" or the "grey" (questionable) areas of tax law. This book is not about tax tricks, "tax avoidance," or "red flags" to get you audited. We are not out to deceive the Internal Revenue Service or anyone else.

These deductions are genuine, acceptable, IRS-approved All American Tax Deductions. And each and every one is Money In Your Pocket That Stays In Your Pocket. If the United States Government says that I am entitled to take a deduction and pay less taxes, by gosh, I consider it my patriotic duty to take that deduction.

Federal Versus State Laws

The laws explained in this book are federal tax laws, for preparing your federal tax return. Many states have the exact same laws as the feds, and most business deductions allowed on your federal return are also allowed on your state return. But that is not guaranteed. You should study the instructions that come with your state tax forms, or state tax publications, or ask your accountant. You might also find additional state deductions that the IRS does not allow, and save even more money on your state taxes.

"I Wish I Had This Book Last Year" (Amending Prior Years' Tax Returns)

Did you miss some deductions on last year's tax return that you were entitled to? Well, as some newspaper woman said many years ago, "Yes Virginia, there is a Santa Claus."

You can go back and amend prior tax returns and claim a refund of prior years' taxes. Amended tax returns must be filed within three years from the date you filed your original return or within two years from the time you paid your tax, whichever is later. A return filed early is considered filed on the due date. So for 2002 tax returns filed and paid on time (April 15, 2003) or ahead of time, you have until the April 15, 2006, to amend the return.

Tax returns are amended on form 1040-X for sole proprietorships, 1120-X for regular corporations, 1120-S (marked "Amended") for S corporations, and 1065 (marked "Amended") for partnerships and Limited Liability Companies. Refunds are fairly prompt.

As to IRS audits of amended returns, my experience is that amended returns are not more likely to be audited than original returns.

If your federal return was in error, your state return was probably also in error. States have similar procedures for amending returns.

Keeping Records

Many legitimate tax deductions are lost because people don't know about them. That's the reason for this book. But many more tax deductions are lost simply because people failed to record them. People who do not keep good records too often cheat themselves out of deductions because they didn't write them down. Record keeping is, in fact, the very heart of taking advantage of tax deductions.

If you don't have a good set of business ledgers, STOP. If you do not have a good system for recording every business expense, STOP. Get a set of ledgers, or get an accounting software program, and learn how to use it. Hire an accountant or a bookkeeper, if necessary, to help you set up the ledgers and teach you the basics. Or read my book *Small Time Operator: How to Start Your Own Business, Keep Your Books, Pay Your Taxes, and Stay Out of Trouble*.

Get receipts for everything you possibly can, set up a good filing system for the receipts, and keep the receipts at least three years. Three years from the date you file your tax return is the IRS statute of limitations for most audits. Receipts are your best proof if the IRS ever challenges a deduction. If you don't have receipts, make notes about expenses, or keep a business diary. Record mileage. And don't forget all those tiny out-of-pocket expenses; even small purchases can add up to a significant tax deduction.

The IRS says that receipts and other business records can be kept on paper or stored electronically, on disk or on your computer, as long as the information can be retrieved if the IRS requests it.

When Can You Take A Deduction?

Most deductions are taken the year you incur the expense. But there are many exceptions to this rule. Some prepaid expenses (including interest and property taxes) must be deducted the year they apply to, regardless of when they are paid. Some expenses must be depreciated, which means they are written off over several years. Inventory (goods for sale) cannot be written off until the inventory is sold. In the list of 422 deductions, any expense that cannot be deducted currently is explained. You will not have to guess if an expense is currently deductible.

Cash Method Versus Accrual Accounting

You must also understand the two basic accounting methods allowed by the IRS, the Cash Method and the Accrual Method, and how each affects expense deductions.

Under the Cash Method of accounting, expenses are recorded when paid. Credit purchases you haven't yet paid for, do not show on Cash Method ledgers and are not deducted on your tax return until paid. The Cash Method (also called "cash basis") does not mean all your transactions are in cash. It refers to how you record your purchases, and what you can deduct on this year's tax return.

Under the Accrual Method, all expenses are recorded whether paid or not. An expense you incur this year but do not pay until next year is recorded as this year's expense and taken as a tax deduction this year, not next year when the bill is paid.

Any business with annual sales of $1 million or less can use either the cash or accrual method of accounting, your choice.

Certain businesses with annual sales between $1 million and $10 million can also choose either method: Service businesses and contractors whose sales of parts and materials are less than 50% of their total income; and custom manufacturers. (Businesses structured as C corporations have a maximum of $5 million instead of $10 million.)

Sales businesses (retailers, wholesalers, distributors, etc.) and regular manufacturers with sales over $1 million a year must use accrual accounting.

Year End Payments

Checks written and mailed or delivered by December 31 can be deducted the year written, even if cashed in the new year.

Bills paid electronically are deducted the year your account is debited. If a bill is paid in December but not processed by your bank until January, the expense cannot be deducted until the next year.

Credit card expenses (MasterCard, VISA, etc.) can be deducted the year incurred, even if paid next year (accrual method businesses only; cash method businesses deduct the expense when paid). But expenses on charge cards issued by individual stores cannot be deducted until paid, for both cash and accrual businesses.

Structuring Transactions to Your Best Tax Advantage

You want to do your very best to be sure every expense of your business becomes a tax deduction, currently or in future years. Often simply the way you structure a deal, or the way you word a contract, or how you describe an expense, can mean the difference between something that is deductible and something that isn't.

Throughout the book, I try to warn you about different expenditures that can be interpreted or structured in different ways, so you'll be able to make the tax laws work for you. And it is perfectly legal. Large corporations hire $300 per hour tax attorneys to do nothing but find ways around the taxes they don't want to pay. You get to buy this book. But don't be afraid to quiz your tax accountant about any expense that may want a little "reworking."

How many times have you heard about some business that is losing money or making a worthless purchase or spending frivolously, but, Hey, it's a tax write off. After over twenty years dealing with tax laws, I still don't find logic in this strategy. The concept of incurring an expense solely as a tax write-off is, when you get right down to it, ridiculous. The expense will always be greater than the tax write off the expense brings, that must be obvious. (A tax "write off" and a tax "deduction" are the same thing).

Business transactions should not be tax motivated. Make sure the deal has a real economic purpose independent of tax consequences. Then figure out how to structure the deal to your best advantage.

Timing Transactions to Your Best Tax Advantage

As the end of the year approaches, you can structure your business transactions to increase or decrease your profit, and therefore increase or decrease the taxes you will pay. Within limits, you can postpone or accelerate purchases and other business expenses.

For example, if you are thinking of buying a new computer, you can buy it in December for a deduction this year, or buy it in January for a deduction next year. You can do same with other office equipment, supplies, repairs, etc.

If you are on the Cash Method of accounting (see above), expenses you pay this year are deductible this year (with some important exceptions). You can prepay some of next year's expenses and get a deduction this year, when you pay the bills, instead of next year. Or you can postpone paying some of this year's bills until next year if you would rather get the deduction next year instead of this year.

If you are on the Accrual Method, you do not have as much flexibility as businesses on the Cash Method, but you can still decide to make a large purchase in December instead of January, or vice versa.

If the current year is a low income year, and if you already have enough deductions to bring your taxes down and keep your tax bracket at the minimum, you would probably benefit from postponing expenses to next year. If, on the other hand, this is a high income year and you could use more deductions to reduce your tax burden, accelerating expenses, spending the money this year instead of next year, may be the best tax strategy. You might want to talk to your accountant in November or early December about your options. Once it's New Year's Day, it's too late.

Equipment, Supplies, and Inventory Owned Before Going Into Business

Items you owned before going into business that get used in the business (converted to business use), are eligible for some but not all of the tax deductions as items purchased specifically for business.

Assets converted to business use must be valued at your cost, or at their market value at the time the assets are first used in your business, whichever is less.

Business assets such as furniture, computer, tools and equipment that were purchased before going into business, can be depreciated using the same depreciation schedules for similar assets. These assets, however, are not eligible for first-year write off (as explained under

"Business Assets" in the main section). They must be depreciated.

Inventory and supplies are deducted exactly the same as inventory and supplies purchased specifically for the business.

If your business is a sole proprietorship, you simply put the items in your business, much as you put your cash in the business.

If the business is a partnership or limited liability company (LLC), you can still put the items in the business, but be careful how you and your business co-owners view the ownership of the items.

If your business is a corporation, you may have to legally transfer ownership to the corporation. This will require help from your accountant.

Partners in Partnerships
Owners of Corporations
Members of Limited Liability Companies

Try not to pay business expenses out of your personal funds. Business deductions are sometimes disallowed when claimed by the business owners or employees, instead of by the companies themselves. If you must pay any business expenses out of your own pocket or from your personal credit card, have the business reimburse you, so the business itself can claim the deductions.

Home Based Businesses

Almost everything in this book applies to home businesses as well as to more conventional businesses. IRS rules, requirements and restrictions, however, are sometimes different for home businesses than for businesses operated outside the home. For each deduction listed in the book, any differences are labeled in bold and explained.

The most significant tax issues that apply only to home-based businesses are the deductions for the business space in the home: the rent if you rent your home, depreciation if you own your home, utilities, maintenance, and other space-related expenses.

Depending on how you set up and how you use your home business, you may or may not be eligible for a deduction for the space used for business. The item **Home Office** in the alphabetical listing of 422 deductions includes complete and detailed information on what home offices (home shops, home stores, home studios, etc.) are eligible for the deduction.

I mention this in the Home Office listing, but it bears repeating: Failure to qualify for the home office deduction doesn't prohibit you from operating your business out of your home. It only means that one possibly large expense is not deductible on your federal income taxes. You can still deduct all legitimate business expenses other than those directly related to the business space itself.

Internet Businesses

Contrary to what many publications report, the Internet is not "tax free." Internet business is subject to the exact same tax laws as all other businesses. The only specific ban on Internet taxes applies to Internet access charges. No state nor the federal government can levy a tax on Internet access charges.

Every Internet business is subject to the federal income tax. Every tax deduction in this book applies to Internet businesses.

One Last Caution

Verify what you read in this book with a current IRS publication or with a competent accountant or attorney. Tax law is like quicksand, it's built on an ever changing foundation. Congress is constantly screwing around with the tax laws. As soon as they pass another confusing law and promptly go on vacation, the IRS starts issuing interpretations of the law. And then some clever tax attorney finds a loophole, and the Tax Court gets to put in its two cents. Pretty soon, the law means something different than it did a few months ago.

The word once printed cannot be altered. Tax law, however, changes constantly. As the carpenter says, "Measure twice, cut once."

Terminology

There are many different terms for the same thing. Ten different businesses in ten different states may have ten different terms for a given business expense. To make this book as easy as possible to use, I have tried to list every term I know for every business deduction.

For example, you can look up "Goodwill" and find that it is also known as "Blue Sky." You can look up "Blue Sky" and find it is also known as "Goodwill." Employee benefits are explained under "Benefits" and "Fringe Benefits." This system results in some repetition and some duplication of definitions and explanations, but I think it makes the book faster and easier for people to use, and it eliminates the need to spend time pouring through an index.

Here are a few important definitions you should know before getting any deeper into this book:

Self Employed Individuals

Throughout this book, you will see the term "self employed individuals." Self employed individuals are in business for themselves. They are owners of sole proprietorships, partners in partnerships, and member/owners of limited liability companies (LLCs).

Independent contractors are self employed individuals. Freelancers, consultants, contractors, free agents and other people in an independent trade or profession are self employed individuals.

There is a very important distinction between the above self employed individuals, and people who have set up their businesses as corporations. People who own corporations, both regular C corporations and S corporations, are employees of their businesses. Although they are obviously self employed, for tax purposes—and for understanding the terminology in this book—they are not called self employed individuals. They are referred to as employees, or if a distinction is important, as owner/employees.

Tax laws for corporations are often different than tax laws for unincorporated businesses: sole proprietorships, partnerships, and limited liability companies. Tax laws for owners of corporations, who are legally employees of their businesses, are often different than tax laws for owners of unincorporated businesses, who are not legally employees of their businesses, but who are self-employed individuals.

In describing the tax deductions in this book, if the deductions are different for different types of businesses or different types of owners, the differences are explained. You will not have to guess if a deduction applies to you.

Employer / Employee

As you go through this book, be very careful reading the last letter of these two words. The employer hires the employee. The employee works for the employer. The employer/ employee relationship is a formal, legal relationship, with very specific tax consequences. Tax deductions for employers are very different than for employees.

Independent contractors, free agents, and other self employed individuals are not employees. If you hire these people, you are not their employer. If you are an independent contractor, the person or company hiring you is not your employer.

This book is very careful to distinguish between employers, employees, and self-employed individuals (non-employees). You are cautioned to be equally careful.

What Is A Tax Deduction?

There are no dumb questions.

A tax deduction is a dollar amount that is subtracted from your total business income (your total sales) in order to arrive at your taxable income, your net profit.

Let's start with some basic tax definitions. Your total income, meaning your total sales for the year, before any deductions, is called "gross income." Gross income does not include loans to the business, money invested in the business, money you put into the business. Gross income is sales, fees, what your customers and clients pay you.

For computing income tax, gross income is first reduced by any "returns," meaning refunds to customers.

Your income is reduced further by the cost of the inventory (goods for sale) sold during the year. This is an expense called "cost of goods sold." It is a tax deduction.

In tax terminology, gross income (total sales), less refunds, less cost of goods sold, is called "gross profit." Note that the terms "gross income" and "gross profit" have different meanings.

Gross profit is reduced by all other allowable business expenses, to arrive at "net profit," which is your taxable profit.

An "allowable business expense" is one the IRS allows to be deducted on your tax return. There are also business expenses, totally legitimate business expenses, that are not allowed by the IRS. The allowable expenses are the tax deductions listed in this book.

An allowable business expense, a tax deduction, is not necessarily money you paid out this year. Some expenses must be deducted over several years. The tax deduction will be spread out over several years even though the cash was paid all in one year.

Some expenses are only partially allowed. You may have a $100 expenditure but only a $50 tax deduction, because only half the expense is allowed by tax law.

So, a tax deduction is what you can deduct, not necessarily what you spent.

This book explains which expenses are fully deductible the year paid, which expenses are deductible over several years, which expenses are only partly deductible, and which expenses are not deductible at all. I have tried to list and explain every possible business expense whether it is deductible or not.

Tax Write Off

A tax write-off is another term for a tax deduction. The two terms are used interchangeably.

"Personal" Vs. Business

A "personal" expense is a non-business expense, and it is not deductible on a business tax return.

However, in tax law, the term "personal" has a second meaning. "Personal property" is any property other than real estate. "Personal property" includes machinery, equipment, furniture, and other assets a business owns. This "personal" property is actually business property, a business expense.

In the book, when I mention a "personal expense," I refer to a non-business expense, not deductible on a business tax return. When I mention "personal property," I am talking about business assets, not non-business assets. This is an important distinction, but you don't have to keep remembering it. Throughout the book, I try to point out the difference as it comes up.

Expenditures that are partly personal (non-business) and partly business can be prorated. The business portion is deductible.

Capitalized Expenses

In tax jargon, the term "capitalize" means that an asset or an expense cannot be deducted immediately. Such items are often called "capital assets" or "capital expenditures."

Some capital assets must be deducted over a period of years, which is usually referred to as "depreciating" or "amortizing" the asset. Buildings and patents are two examples of assets that must be "capitalized" and depreciated over many years.

Some capital assets cannot be deducted until sold. Land is an example of an asset that must be "capitalized" and not deducted until sold.

Assets and expenses that must be capitalized are explained in the item list.

Audits

Throughout the book, I discuss IRS audits. I warn you about any deductions that might trigger IRS audits, and potential audit situations you should discuss with your accountant. So, what exactly is an IRS audit?

Every year, the IRS selects a small percentage of business tax returns to examine, looking to prove that the returns are accurate, that income is honestly stated, that deductions are legal. The IRS agents accomplish this task by talking to you or your accountant, by looking at your business ledgers, and by examining your bank statements and business receipts.

Some audits are extensive, some are narrowly focused. Some audits will cover your entire business operation for the year, some audits may question only one or a few deductions.

At the conclusion of the audit, the IRS will report their findings to you and let you know if your tax bill increased, decreased, or remained unchanged.

Quite often, the IRS will find an error on a tax return when processing the return, typically an adding mistake or a tax calculation mistake. The IRS will automatically correct your return and notify you of your error and the increase or decrease in taxes. This kind of correction is not an audit. It does not increase or decrease your chances of being audited.

By the way, the term "audit" is no longer officially used by the IRS. According to the latest IRS press release, the IRS no longer "audits" tax returns. They, ah, "conduct examinations." The "examinations," however, are identical to what the IRS used to call "audits." Why the euphemism, I do not know. What I do know is, Fish is fish. An audit is an audit. And part of the goal of this book is to help you avoid an audit.

Tax Credits Vs. Tax Deductions

Tax credits are also listed in this book. Tax credits are different than tax deductions. A tax deduction reduces your net profit from your business. A tax credit does not reduce your net business profit, but it does reduce your income taxes. What is the difference?

You compute your business profit (your net profit) by taking your total income and subtracting from it your tax deductions, as explained above. You figure your tax based on this net profit.

After you compute your taxes, you then use any allowable tax credits to reduce those taxes. Again, a tax credit does not reduce your profit, it reduces the taxes on the profit.

For example, let's say you have a taxable profit of $20,000 for the year. If you are in, say, a 15% tax bracket, your income taxes are $3,000: 15% of $20,000. (I know that's simplifying tax calculations tremendously, but it makes the example a lot easier to explain).

Then you read this book and find a $1,000 tax deduction you didn't know about. So you are able to write off an additional $1,000. Your profits are now $19,000 instead of $20,000 and your taxes are $2,850 instead of $3,000. (15% of $19,000 is $2,850). That $1,000 tax deduction saved you $150 in income taxes.

If instead, the $1,000 you found by reading this book was a tax credit instead of a tax deduction, the computations are different. The tax credit does not reduce your profit. So you still have a $20,000 profit and a $3,000 tax bill. But then you reduce the $3,000 in taxes by the full $1,000 credit. Your taxes are now $2,000.

If you were able to follow this slightly confusing example, you'll see that a tax credit is more valuable than a tax deduction. In our example, the $1,000 tax deduction saved you $150 in taxes, but the $1,000 tax credit saved you a full $1,000 in taxes. The tax credit is a little gold mine, it is.

An item is either a tax deduction or a tax credit, not both.

Why does Congress offer both tax deductions and tax credits? To confuse the issues, of course. To make life more complicated for people trying to figure their taxes. To make accountants and tax lawyers rich. And because no one in Congress does his own tax return and has no idea how confusing the tax laws are. That's why.

That's not why. Most tax deductions are actual business expenses, the actual costs of running a business. Tax deductions tend to stay the same, year after year. Many tax credits have nothing to do with the actual expense of running a business. They are instead tax breaks to encourage you to do socially responsible things like hire people off of welfare, or to purchase equipment that will make for cleaner air and water. Some tax credits are meant to stimulate the economy. And some, believe it or not, just give you a much needed tax break, period. Send a letter of thanks to your Congressman or Congresswoman for the self-employment tax credit, the health insurance tax credit, tuition tax credit, research and development tax credit, oil drilling tax credit (that's right), and whatever else they've given us (or their corporate buddies) for Christmas this year.

Unlike tax deductions, tax credits tend to come and go, available one year and not the next. Congress has discovered that it is much easier to yank a tax credit they want to be rid of, than it is to drop a long-time tax deduction, which has been engraved on the stone tablets of tax law.

There is one more important difference between tax deductions and tax credits. Since tax deductions reduce your business profit, they also reduce your self-employment tax (Social Security and Medicare tax for self-employed individuals), which is approximately 15% of your profit. Tax credits, however, do not reduce your profit. So tax credits do not reduce your self-employment tax.

There are very few tax credits, every one specifically spelled out in tax law. By comparison, there are hundreds and hundreds of tax deductions, many of them not even mentioned in the IRS Tax Code, tax books, or tax forms at all.

In this book, tax credits are specifically labeled as such. If an item in this book does not say it is a tax credit, it is a tax deduction. If it doesn't say whether it is a tax deduction or a tax credit, it is a tax deduction. Read carefully.

Basic Rules: All Expenses

Some business tax deductions are specifically spelled out in the IRS Tax Code: yes, you can deduct this, no you cannot deduct that. But the great majority of business deductions, most of the 422 tax deductions listed in this book, are not mentioned anywhere in the IRS code books. The law does not say, for example, that you can or cannot deduct pens for the office, or light bulbs for the warehouse, or bank service charges.

What the IRS does say, and says very adamantly, is that all business expenses—and I mean *all* expenses, whether spelled out in the IRS code books or not—must meet four basic rules in order to be deductible:

1. The expenses must be incurred in connection with your trade, business, or profession.
2. The expenses must be "ordinary."
3. The expenses must be "necessary."
4. The expenses must "not be lavish or extravagant under the circumstances."

Any expense that cannot meet all four of these requirements cannot be deducted on your business tax return.

The four basic rules, however, are not always as basic as they sound. (Of course...) It is important for every business owner to understand a little more about these rules and, most important, to understand the definitions of the words as they are used in tax law.

I am not going to confuse you here. These definitions, these tax laws, are not difficult to understand. If you will take five minutes to read these definitions, you will have a much greater understanding of tax law, and what you can legitimately deduct on your tax return.

Rule One: The expenses must be incurred in connection with your trade, business, or profession.

The words "trade," "business," and "profession" are used interchangeably. All three refer to an activity carried on with a reasonable degree of regularity, and with the sincere attempt to make a profit. It includes all self-employed individuals, sole proprietors, partners, members (owners) of Limited Liability Companies (LLCs), freelancers, independent contractors, free agents, independent professionals. It includes full time, part time, seasonal, and home business operators. It includes Internet businesses.

"Reasonable degree of regularity" rules out occasional activities that bring in a little income. Such occasional activities are not considered a trade or business by the IRS. "Sincere attempt to make a profit" rules out hobbies and other ventures done purely or mostly for the fun of it. There must be a real profit motive or the IRS says it is not a trade or business.

The expression "in connection with your trade or business" also means that you have already started a business. You must actually be in business before you are allowed to write off business expenses. You are not allowed a deduction for business expenses incurred in connection with a trade or business you are thinking of starting, planning to start some day, or researching in anticipation of starting.

There is a real problem here for people who are genuinely getting ready to open a business but haven't yet opened the doors or gone looking for their first customer. The IRS calls any pre-opening expenses "start up costs," and there are specific rules for deducting such costs. Deductions are limited and sometimes completely disallowed for some start-up costs. The rules are explained under the heading "Start Up Costs" in the main section of this book. Before you incur any start-up costs, you should read the Start-Up Costs listing to find out how you can maximize your deductions.

Expenditures that are partly personal (non-business) and partly business can be prorated. The business portion is deductible. Any asset that you originally purchased and used for non-business purposes that you are now using for business or using partly for business is deductible.

Method of Payment: Method of payment is immaterial. Payment can be made by cash, check, money order, credit card, or debit (cash) card. If your business is a sole proprietorship, you can pay business expenses with a personal (non-business) check, credit card or debit card and get a business deduction. A business expense is deductible even if paid by a non-business check or credit card. But if you own a corporation or are in a partnership or limited liability company, the business should pay the bills. If you pay business expenses, the business should reimburse you.

Who the bill is made out to is also immaterial. If an invoice or a bill for a business expense is made out to you personally, instead of to your business, you still get a business deduction if the expense is a business expense.

Special note to investors: Investing money—in other businesses, securities, commodities, the stock market—is not considered a trade or business by the IRS. Although people do invest with a "reasonable degree of regularity" and with the "sincere attempt to make a profit," investing does not meet the IRS definition of a trade or business. Sorry, you bought the wrong book. (This does not apply to people investing in their own businesses. You did buy the right book).

Rule Two: The expenses must be "ordinary."

"Ordinary" expenses are ones that are common or accepted in your type of business. They do not have to be recurring or habitual.

Rule Three: The expenses must be "necessary."

A "necessary" expense, according to the IRS, is one "that is appropriate and helpful in developing and maintaining your trade or business."

It's important to understand that the word "necessary" in this context of IRS tax law, does not have the same definition we usually associate with "necessary," as in "required," "indispensable," "must be done." It is not *necessary* that you buy nice stationery. It is not *necessary* that you air condition your office. These are not mandatory requirements of your business, but they pass the "necessary" test. An expense only has to be "appropriate and helpful" to meet the "necessary" test.

Rule Four: The expenses must "not be lavish or extravagant under the circumstances."

Defining what is or is not "lavish or extravagant under the circumstances" depends on, well, depends on the circumstances. The bigger the business and the more income the business earns, the more likely you can deduct large amounts of money and call the expenses "not lavish or extravagant under the circumstances." Full time, ongoing businesses can usually get away with a bit more lavish-ness than part time and new businesses.

What if you are only working part time, or just getting started? What if you have only a few clients? Would the IRS consider an expensive business trip extravagant? Most likely, an IRS agent would be inclined to disallow such a deduction. But there is no clear answer to this question.

My own guideline: if you think the deductions might be consid-ered lavish or extravagant, there is a good likelihood they are. This is an area where I strongly advise you to get professional advice from a competent tax accountant.

There is no question that all four basic requirements are sometimes vague and subject to interpretation. The IRS, fortunately, tends to be quite reasonable about what's reasonable ("not lavish or extravagant"), as well as what is "ordinary" and "necessary." If the expense is business related, if it isn't outrageously extravagant, if it doesn't stick out on your tax return like a tuba in a string quartet, you are probably okay. And remember, try to get receipts for every-thing, and keep them.

422 Tax Deductions

From "Accountants" to "Zoning," these 422 listings are arranged in alphabetical order. Each deduction is defined and explained. Cross references are in bold typeface. Special situations (such as rules specific to home businesses, manufacturers, corporations, employers, etc.) are labeled in bold and explained. The "Expense Category" suggests where to put the deduction on your tax form.

This alphabetical listing also includes tax credits, which are different than tax deductions (explained in the Introduction); and business expenses that are not deductible—just so you'll know.

Anyone may so arrange his affairs that his taxes shall be as low as possible. He is not bound to choose that pattern which best pays the Treasury. Everyone does it, rich and poor alike, and all do right. For nobody owes any public duty to pay more than the law demands.

—Judge Learned Hand

Accountants

It figures that the very first entry would be "accountants."

Accountants' fees are deductible. Business consultations with your accountant are deductible. Accounting, bookkeeping, payroll, tax return preparation, auditing, tax advice and similar services are all deductible. Cost of hiring an accountant to help you with an IRS audit are deductible.

For preparing the tax return of a sole proprietor, only the cost of preparing the business part of the 1040 tax return (schedule C and related schedules) is deductible as a business expense. You should ask your accountant to separate out the fees for the business and personal parts of your tax return.

One important exception to the deductibility of accounting and other professional fees: Expenses incurred before starting your business and expenses associated with buying a business come under special rules. See **Start Up Costs. Buying a Business**.

Expense category: Legal and professional services.

Small businesses are very unhappy with the IRS. And I don't blame them.
—*IRS Commissioner Charles O. Rossotti*

Accident Insurance

Accident insurance comes under the same rules as Health Insurance. See **Health Insurance**.

(Yes, I know, Accident should come before Accountant, but I did not want to start the book with "Accident.")

Advances

Advances paid to contractors, professionals, vendors, etc. are deductible.

If the advance is a prepayment for work not yet done or goods not yet delivered, if the advance is a substantial amount of money, and if the advance applies to goods or services to be received next year, the deduction may have to be postponed to next year. See **Prepayments.**

If an advance is later refunded to you, and if you've already taken a deduction for it, you must reduce your current expenses or increase you gross income by the amount of the refund. Either way, the net effect is the same: to reverse the deduction you originally claimed.

Some advances are called deposits, but advances and deposits are not always the same thing. Generally, refundable deposits are not deductible. Non-refundable deposits are deductible. But like advances, deposits that are actually prepayments of some expense come under the prepaid expense rules. See **Prepayments.**

Expense category: Varies depending on actual expenses.

Advances to employees are considered regular taxable wages, subject to all payroll and withholding taxes.

Expense category: Wages.

A tax is a compulsory payment for which no specific benefit is received in return.

—U.S. Treasury

Advertising

Advertising and promotional expenses are deductible. Advertising materials such as flyers and catalogs are also deductible. Sometimes the term "promotion" is also called "entertainment." But promotion and advertising expenses are fully deductible, and entertainment is limited to a 50% deduction. Be careful how you define your expenses.

Expense category: Advertising.

Aircraft

Aircraft can be deducted the year of purchase, with limitations, or depreciated. See **Business Assets** and **Depreciation**.

Expense category: Depreciation. You must also fill out Form 4562, "Depreciation and Amortization."

The cost of operating business aircraft used by employees for personal trips may be restricted (according to the IRS) or may be fully deductible (according to the Tax Courts). I suggest you talk to your accountant about this. This is one deduction that invites IRS audits.

Air Fare

Deductible if certain requirements are met. See **Travel**.

Alarms

Alarm systems can be deducted or depreciated like other business assets. See **Business Assets**. If the system is an integral part of the building, it may have to be depreciated along with the building. See **Depreciation**. Monthly service charges and alarm rentals are fully deductible.

Expense category: Rent or lease (rent of a system). Office expense (service charges). Depreciation, and you must also fill out Form 4562, "Depreciation and Amortization" (purchased system).

The current tax system is an unwieldy, inefficient, ungodly mess.
—Former IRS Commissioner Shirley Peterson

Allowance for Bad Debts

An allowance for bad debts, funds set aside in anticipation of a bad debt, is not deductible. Actual bad debts are deductible. See **Bad Debts**.

Amortization

Intangible assets such as trademarks and patents must be deducted over a period of years. The deduction is called amortization. It is similar to depreciation, and the procedure is the same. See **Depreciation**.

Expense category: Depreciation. You must also fill out Form 4562, "Depreciation and Amortization."

If you acquire rights to a trademark from another business, under a licensing agreement, the payments are deductible when paid. They do not have to be amortized.

Expense category: Other expenses.

The term amortization also refers to paying off a loan. Loan amortization is not a deductible expense. A loan is not income when you get it and is not an expense when you pay it off. Any interest is deductible. See **Interest**.

Answering Service

Telephone answering service fees are deductible. Any initial setup or installation charges are also deductible.

Expense category: Office expense; or Legal & professional services.

Government in the United States today is a senior partner in every business in the country.

—Norman Cousins

Antiques

Valuable antiques and art treasures, if used for decoration only, may not be depreciated and cannot be deducted until sold.

Antiques actually used in the business, such as an old desk, or a professional musician's rare violin, can be depreciated or, at your option, deducted the year of purchase (up to a maximum amount), but only if the items can wear out or deteriorate from use. See **Business Assets** and **Depreciation**.

I should warn you that the above deduction rule comes from a Tax Court case, fought and lost by the IRS. The IRS continues to state that no rare and valuable antiques can be written off until sold, regardless of how they are used. If you have significant money at stake here, I suggest you talk to your accountant.

Expense category: Depreciation. You must also fill out Form 4562, "Depreciation and Amortization."

Appraisal Fees

Appraisal fees paid to determine the amount of a loss are deductible. Appraisal fees paid to determine a value on a donated item are deductible (for corporations only—see **Donations**). Real estate appraisal fees are deductible. Appraisal fees involving the purchase or sale of a business may have to be capitalized (deducted over several years). See **Start-Up Costs**.

Expense category: Legal and professional services.

Art Treasures

Art treasures and decorative antiques are not deductible. The IRS states that these objects do not depreciate in value, so no deduction or depreciation allowed. You report a profit or loss on the items when you sell them.

Dealers in antiques and art treasures, however, treat these items as inventory. See **Inventory**.

Assessments

Local government assessments for repair (not construction) of streets, sidewalks, water lines, sewers and the like are deductible.

Expense category: Taxes and licenses.

Assessments for improvements that increase the value of your property are not deductible. The expense must be added to the cost of your property and depreciated. These assessments include new construction of streets, sidewalks, water and sewer lines. See **Depreciation.**

Expense category: Depreciation. You must also fill out Form 4562, "Depreciation and Amortization."

The American War of Independence had its origin in the refusal to pay taxes imposed by Britain. Constitutional scholars argue to this day whether the framers of the Constitution ruled out or allowed an income tax. The framers' wisdom is clothed in ambiguity. But for 85 years, no income tax was ever considered, until the government ran short of funds during the Civil War. The Act of Congress of August 5, 1861 imposed a 3% federal income tax. The Supreme Court ruled it unconstitutional. Congress, bound and determined to have an income tax, voted 318 to 14 for the Sixteenth Amendment in 1909. It was ratified by the states on February 15, 1913. Six years later in 1919, the Intelligence Unit of the United States Treasury Department was created, for the general purpose of preventing tax evasion. The name was later changed to the Internal Revenue Service.
        —*"The Law and the Profits," by Prof. C. Northcote Parkinson*

Associations

Dues and other expenses for business groups, professional organizations, merchant and trade associations, chambers of commerce, etc. are deductible. Dues to community service organizations, such as Rotary, Lions, etc., are also deductible.

Expense category: Other expenses.

Dues and membership fees in clubs run for pleasure, recreation, or other social purposes are not deductible. These include athletic, luncheon, hotel, airline, sporting, and other entertainment or recreational organizations, associations, clubs and facilities. Even if you use a club membership solely to generate or discuss business, the dues are not deductible. Sometimes the term "business club" is used to describe such a facility. If the "business" club is not a business organization, the dues are not deductible.

Athletic Facilities

Athletic and recreation facilities on the business premises which are open to all employees are deductible. Equipment can be deducted the year of purchase (up to a maximum amount) or depreciated. Structures and built-in structural components have to be depreciated. See **Business Assets** and **Depreciation**.

Expense category: Depreciation. You must also fill out Form 4562, "Depreciation and Amortization."

Dues and membership fees to athletic clubs are not deductible.

Attorneys

A business owner was getting 20 minutes of advice from his lawyer. When the time was up, the businessman paid the lawyer the $100 he owed. As the businessman was leaving, the lawyer discovered that a second $100 bill had accidentally stuck to the first one. The lawyer found himself in a moral dilemma: should he tell his partner?

The $100 the businessman thought he paid was deductible. Actually, $200 was deductible. He lost coming and going.

Expense category: Legal and professional services.

Audits

The cost of an audit by an accounting firm or auditing service is deductible. The cost of hiring an accountant or lawyer to defend yourself in an IRS audit of your business is deductible. Any additional taxes or penalties are not deductible.

Interest on back taxes is not deductible (except for corporations), according to the IRS. Some Tax Courts disagree.

Expense category: Legal and professional services.

Lots of things can happen if you don't keep the right records, and none of them are good.

—C.P.A. Dan Smogor

Automobiles

Cars used for business can be deducted or depreciated, but with certain limitations. See **Vehicles**.

Expense category: The category "Car and truck expenses" is for all vehicle expenses except the cost of the vehicle itself, which is deducted or depreciated under "Depreciation." See **Depreciation**.

Leased automobiles: Automobile leases, if 30 days or longer, are not 100% deductible. The IRS has a table called "Inclusion Amounts for Cars" that shows how much of an auto lease can be deducted. See IRS Publication 463 for the table. This rules does not apply to trucks, vans or heavy sport utility vehicles.

If Patrick Henry thought that taxation without representation was bad, he should see how bad it is with representation.

—*Farmer's Almanac*

Awards

Awards to employees: Awards (and prizes and bonuses) paid to employees are considered wages subject to all payroll taxes. Awards are deductible like all employee wages. Small token awards of merchandise—not cash—to employees are not taxable to the employee.)

However, the IRS recognizes something they call an "employee achievement award." As much as $1,600 per year can be given to an employee, tax free, as an employee achievement award, and the employer gets a deduction. Employee achievement awards are for length of service or for safety, but not for things like top salesperson of the month or extra hours worked. Employee achievement awards must not be "disguised compensation."

There is an important distinction between an award and a gift. See **Business Gifts**.

Expense category: Wages

Awards to non-employees are fully deductible.
Expense category: Advertising, or Other expenses.

Bad Checks

Deductible. See **Bounced Checks**.
Expense category: Bad debts.

We hang the petty thieves, but appoint the great ones to public office.
—Aesop, 600 B.C.

Bad Debts

Bad debts are deductible. These include customers' bounced checks and credit card charges customers refuse to pay.

If you sell on account to customers, any uncollectible accounts are deductible, but only if they were posted to your income ledger when you made the sale. Businesses using the cash method of accounting (recording income when the money comes in, not when the sale was made) cannot take a bad debt expense for uncollectible accounts, because the income was not recorded in the first place.

If this sounds confusing, understand that tax law says that if you don't get paid for work performed or goods sold, you don't report any income. You get a bad debt deduction only if you recorded income in your income ledger that you are unable to collect. Whatever income you recorded in your income ledger that is not collectible, the same amount is recorded as a bad debt deduction.

A self-employed individual cannot take a bad debt deduction for his or her own time devoted to a client or customer who doesn't pay. Again, you get a bad debt deduction only if you posted the income to your income ledger. The bad debt deduction in effect reverses out the income you cannot collect. You do not get an additional deduction for the income you should have earned, the money you were cheated out of. I know that doesn't sound fair, and it isn't, but that is how the tax laws are written. You are out the money you should have earned, and the IRS says, Tough Luck.

You do get a deduction for any inventory (goods) you sold that you didn't get paid for. Inventory is deducted at the end of the year as part of cost-of-goods-sold. See **Inventory**.

Deduct only those bad debts that you are certain are uncollectible.

If you are unsure, you can wait until next year. You can write off a bad debt in any future year that it becomes definitely uncollectible.

Expense category: Bad debts.

Bad Debt Reserves: A few businesses that anticipate large bad debts sometimes set aside money in a bad debt reserve fund, sort of like self-insurance. Such reserves are not really business expenses and are not tax deductible.

Taxpayers and tax preparers have lost faith in the fairness of the Internal Revenue Code, and therefore, the Government implementing that code. This is especially true for the lower and middle income taxpayer, both businesses and individuals. These inequities in our voluntary tax system are generally perpetuated because of Congress's tendency to enact legislation that is burdensome, unfair and economically unsound.

—C.P.A. Vern Hoven, Vern Hoven Tax Seminars

Bail Bond Fees

Some business-related bail bond fees may be deductible, if they meet the IRS's "Ordinary" and "Necessary" tests. You should ask your accountant about this. Bail bond fees are not legal fines or legal penalties, which are not deductible.

Expense category: Legal and professional services.

Bank Charges

Bank charges, services, penalties, check writing and credit card fees, are deductible. Check printing costs are deductible.

Expense category: Office expenses.

Bankruptcy

Cost of filing for bankruptcy and related expenses are deductible.

Expense category: Legal and professional services.

If one of your customers files for bankruptcy, and you are unable to collect money owed to you, you will have a bad debt expense, deductible unless you are on the cash basis of accounting. See **Bad Debts**. Any expenses you incur to try to collect the debts are deductible. If a supplier goes bankrupt, and if you have paid for goods or services not delivered, you can deduct your loss as a bad debt.

Expense category: Bad debts.

Bar and Restaurant "Smallware"

Deductible, but see **Restaurant and Bar Smallware**.

The federal tax code is a disgrace to the human race.
                                        —Former President Jimmy Carter

If he felt that way about it, why didn't he attempt to make some changes?
                                        —Tax columnist Carl Kyle

---

Barter

"In the beginning, there was no money." But there always was the tax man, and barter does not escape his grasp. Barter transactions are taxable just like all other business transactions.

When you exchange or trade your business goods or services for someone else's goods or services, it is called barter. The "fair market value" of the goods or services you receive must be included in your regular business income and treated just like any other business income. "Fair market value" is what you would have normally paid for the goods or services in the normal course of business ("arm's length transaction"), had you been paying cash.

If the goods or services you receive are used in your business, you get a business deduction on your taxes, just as though you paid cash. You deduct the fair market value of the goods or services received.

If you join a barter club (exchange, network), the rules are basically the same. Barter club commissions and fees are also deductible.

Barter clubs report all transactions to the IRS. In IRS audits of businesses, one of the first questions often asked is, "Do you engage in trade or barter?" A yes answer is a red flag to expand the scope of the audit to include items of unreported income.

Expense category: Depends on what is acquired in trade.

Benefits

Employers can deduct the cost of employee fringe benefits, with some exceptions and limits. Fringe benefits for you, the owner of the business, and for your family may or may not be deductible depending on how your business is structured.

See: **Awards, Business Gifts, Dependent Care, Discounts, Education, Health Insurance, Life Insurance, Medical Expenses, Medical Savings Accounts, Parking, Retirement Plans.**

Expense category: Employee benefit programs.

Government is a reality of life. Denying it is just letting your own biases influence your business judgment. —Bill McGowan, founder, MCI

Billboards

Rental costs for billboards are deductible. Billboards you own can be deducted (up to a maximum amount) or depreciated.

See **Business Assets, Depreciation**.

Expense category: Rent or lease; or Depreciation (you must also fill out Form 4562, "Depreciation and Amortization").

Blue Sky

Another term for goodwill, an intangible asset. If purchased as part of the purchase price of a business, it must be amortized (depreciated) over a period of years. See **Goodwill**.

Expense category: Depreciation. You must also fill out Form 4562, "Depreciation and Amortization."

From 1900 to 1998, the U.S. population grew from 76 million to 275 million. The federal budget grew from $550 million to $1.7 trillion. The federal income tax grew from zero to $749 billion.

—Reported by the National Chamber of Congress

Boats

Boats, if needed for your business, can be deducted the year of purchase, with limitations, or depreciated. See **Business Assets** and **Depreciation**. Boats used for recreation or entertainment are usually not deductible.

Expense category: Depreciation. You must also fill out Form 4562, "Depreciation and Amortization."

Bodyguard

(1) If needing a bodyguard is an ordinary and necessary expense of your business, it is a deductible expense. (2) If needing a bodyguard is an ordinary and necessary expense of your business, I would suggest you start a different business.

Expense category: Other Expenses.

Bonds

There is a type of insurance called a surety bond. If you do not complete a job, for any reason, your surety company must do so. Many service businesses such as auto repair shops and many building contractors are required by law to have surety bonds. The cost of surety bonds is deductible.

There is a type of insurance called a fidelity bond. Fidelity bonds are placed on employees, insuring against theft or embezzlement by the bonded employees. If you have employees going into people's homes and businesses, such as a janitorial service, a fidelity bond protects you and the client should one of your employees turn out to be a thief. The cost of fidelity bonds is deductible.

Expense category: Insurance.

There are monetary documents called bonds, interest bearing instruments (as they are often called) similar to notes or loans. The bonds themselves are not deductible. The interest is deductible.

Expense category: Interest.

I don't think government officials are against small business. They just have other priorities.

—Jere Glover, U.S. Small Business Administration

Bonus

Bonuses paid to employees are considered wages subject to all payroll taxes and laws. Bonuses are deductible, like all employee wages. Also see **Awards**.

Expense category: Wages.

There is an important distinction between a bonus and a gift. A bonus is a payment for services performed by the employee. A gift is, well, a gift. Gift deductions are limited to a maximum cost of $25 per recipient per year, and are not taxable to the employee.

Expense category: Other Expenses.

Bookkeeping

Bookkeeping, accounting, and similar services are deductible.

Cost of preparing business tax returns is fully deductible. For sole proprietors, only the cost of preparing the business part of your 1040 tax return (schedule C and related schedules) is deductible as a business expense.

Expense category: Legal and professional services.

Books

Books, magazines, newsletters, newspapers, and all other publications are deductible. The cost of buying and maintaining your books (ledgers) is deductible.

Expense category: Office expenses.

Every year, an estimated $150 billion, in the form of direct federal subsidies is funneled to large American corporations. Critics call it corporate welfare. It's more than all of the annual payments for Aid to Families with Dependent Children (AFDC), student aid, housing assistance, food and nutrition, and all direct public assistance combined.

—Reported by The Boston Globe

It's corporate welfare of the worst kind.

—House Majority Leader Richard Armey

Bounced Checks

Bounced checks are deductible; that is, the ones your lousy customers bounce on you.

Expense category: Bad debts.

Your own bounced checks, the ones you wrote, are not deductible. Because nothing was actually paid, right? (That makes sense, doesn't it?) The bank charges and penalties are deductible.

Expense category: Office expense.

54

Boxes

Boxes, cartons, and other containers and packaging materials that hold the goods you sell, are considered part of your inventory and must be included in cost of goods sold. See **Inventory**. If, however, the cost of the boxes is not significant or if used only occasionally, most businesses deduct the costs currently as shipping supplies.

Expense category: Supplies.

Bribes

It is illegal to bribe a U.S. public official. It is also illegal to offer a bribe to win a foreign contract. Illegal payments are not deductible.

But is it illegal to bribe a company official, a purchasing agent, a sales rep, an official or agent of a foreign government? That depends on your state's laws. States have all kinds of laws you never knew existed. If a bribe is legal in your state, a legal bribe is deductible. If the bribe is illegal in your state, no deduction.

Business gifts, however, are deductible, up to $25 each (see **Business Gifts**). Is a gift a bribe? Is a bribe a gift? As Professor Clinton once said, "Don't ask, don't tell."

Expense category: Bury it somewhere.

Broker's Fees

A broker's fee to buy or sell real estate usually must be added to the value of the real estate. A broker's fee as part of buying or selling a business usually must be added to the cost of the business. Both of the above situations will probably require the help of an accountant.

Any other broker's fee paid in the normal course of business (other than the two situations above) is deductible.

Expense category: Legal and professional services.

Who Gets Welfare, Item #14: Last year, Sunkist Growers received $10 million in taxpayers' money from the U.S. Department of Agriculture, to pay for advertising its products abroad.   —Reported by Women's International League for Peace and Freedom, Philadelphia, Pa.

Buildings

Buildings, and major improvements to buildings, must be depreciated. See **Depreciation**. Some bulk storage facilities can be written off the year of purchase.

The land under the building cannot be depreciated or deducted. You get no tax deduction until you sell the land.

Home-Based Businesses: You can depreciate a percentage of your home if you own your home, but only if you are eligible for the Home Office deduction. See **Home Office**. Home-office depreciation is reported on Form #8829, "Expenses for Business Use of Your Home."

Rehabilitation Tax Credit. If you are rehabilitating a certified historic building or a building built before 1936, for use in your business, you may be eligible for a special tax credit, in addition to the regular depreciation deduction. See **Tax Credits.**

Disabled Access Credit. If you renovate your workplace to accommodate people with disabilities, you may be eligible for a special tax credit, in addition to the regular depreciation deduction. See **Tax Credits.**

Real estate developers: Pre-development costs such as planning and design, blueprints, building permits, engineering studies, landscape plans, and the like, cannot be deducted currently, but must be capitalized.

A fine is a tax for doing something wrong. A tax is a fine for doing something right. —Malcolm St. Pier

---

Business Assets

Tangible business assets such as machinery, equipment, tools, furniture, fixtures, display cases, office machines, and vehicles, can (with some exceptions) be deducted the year of purchase. The total deduction under this rule, all assets combined, cannot exceed $24,000 in any one year (calendar year: January through December, 2002.) This is often referred to as the "first year write off" or the "Section 179 Deduction" (referring to a section in the Internal Revenue Code).

Both new and used assets qualify as long as they were purchased for the business and not before going into business. Assets used in your business that were purchased before going into business must be depreciated. See **Depreciation**.

There are many restrictions to this first-year-write-off rule:

1. This write-off rule does not apply to intangible assets such as patents, copyrights, trademarks, goodwill, software, etc.

2. This rule does not apply to buildings (two exceptions: single-purpose livestock and horticultural structures can be written off; some bulk storage facilities can be written off).

3. This rule does not apply to inventory, parts, manufacturing supplies, office supplies, or other consumables.

4. Married couples are allowed a maximum deduction of $24,000 (2002 maximum) between them.

5. If you have more than one unincorporated business, the $24,000 (2002) is the maximum for all combined businesses.

6. If you purchase more than $200,000 in depreciable assets in any one year, the $24,000 (2002) maximum is reduced, dollar for dollar, by the amount in excess of $200,000. So if you spend $202,000 on depreciable assets this year, the maximum you can write off is $22,000 (that's $2,000 less than the $24,000). If you spend $224,000 or more, no deduction is allowed.

7. The deduction cannot exceed the total taxable income from all unincorporated businesses and salaries combined (both husband and wife if filing jointly). Any deduction disallowed because of this limitation can be carried forward to the next year, and future years if

necessary, until the assets are fully written off. To get the carry forward, you must elect the deduction the year the assets are acquired.

8. If an asset is used partly for business and partly for non-business use, business use must be over 50% to be eligible for this deduction. Assets used 50% or less for business must be depreciated (business portion only).

9. Automobiles, even if used 100% for business, have a maximum deduction different from other assets under this law. The maximum applies to autos but not to trucks, vans, or heavy sport utility vehicles.

10. Assets converted to business use, owned before going into business, are not eligible.

11. If you sell assets you've previously deducted, or convert them to non-business use, you may have to "recapture" the amount you deducted (add it back into income) the year of sale or conversion, depending on how many years you own the asset.

Assets ineligible for this first-year-write-off, or in excess of the maximums, must be depreciated. See **Depreciation**.

This first-year-write-off is optional. If you prefer, you can depreciate some or all of these assets over a period of years rather than deducting them the year of purchase. If you owe little or no income tax this year, it might be worth depreciating the assets, spreading the deduction over several years to get a better tax savings in the future.

See IRS Publication 946, "How to Depreciate Property."

Expense category: Depreciation. You must also fill out Form 4562, "Depreciation and Amortization."

We're not perfect.
—Gene Goldenberg, Publisher, Kiplinger's TaxCut software

The awful truth is that every program is defective. There is no product out there that doesn't have bugs. Our favorite flub was a Parsons Tax Mate bug that always printed the total tax owed as zero.   —PC World Magazine

---

Business Associations

Dues and meetings are deductible. See: **Dues. Travel. Meals. Lodging.**

Expense category: Other expenses.

Business Cards

Business cards are deductible.

Expense category: Office expense.

Business Gifts

Tax deductions for business gifts are limited to $25 per recipient in any one year. Gifts to business entities (such as a gift to a corporation), if not given to specific individuals, are fully deductible; no $25 maximum.

Samples of your merchandise, given to prospective buyers or to people who might review or publicize your products, are not considered gifts and are not subject to these gift limitations. You write off the cost of the free samples (not the retail or market value) as part of cost-of-goods-sold. See **Inventory.**

See IRS Publ. 463, "Travel, Entertainment, Gift & Car Expenses."

Expense category: Other expenses.

Gifts to employees: Money, "cash equivalents" (such as gift certificates), and items of significant value, are considered taxable wages, subject to payroll taxes. Small gifts, such as a Thanksgiving turkey or a birthday gift, are deductible and are not considered part of the employee's wages. Gifts to employees are not subject to the $25 limit.

Expense category: Wages (if wages); or Other expenses (if gifts).

---

*In Seventeen Hundred Seventy Six, A group of American mavericks
Renounced the yoke of tyranny, The tax on stamps, the tax on tea
Our fathers felt that we were fit, To tax ourselves and you'll admit
We have been very good at it.*

—Howard Dietz

Business Licenses

Business licenses, registrations, and similar fees are deductible. *Expense category:* Taxes and licenses.

Business Trips

Business trips are usually deductible. See **Travel**. *Expense category:* Travel.

Busses

Busses and large transporters used for business can be deducted or depreciated like other vehicles. Vehicles have special limitations. See **Vehicles**.

Expense category: The category "Car and truck expenses" is for all vehicle expenses except the cost of the vehicle itself, which is deducted or depreciated under "Depreciation" (you must also fill out Form 4562, "Depreciation and Amortization").

The present system will not be abolished until all the members of Congress are forced to fill out their tax returns alone, without the help of an accountant. —Nicholas Von Hoffman

---

Buying A Business

When you buy someone else's business, the expense deductions get complicated. Some of the purchase price is deductible, some must be depreciated or amortized over several years, some of the cost may not be deductible at all. A lot depends on how the business is structured legally (corporation, partnership, limited liability company, or sole proprietorship) and what the purchase agreement says. The precise legal wording can affect how the sale is taxed, how the assets are valued for tax purposes, and how much of the purchase price will be deductible. You should talk to an experienced tax professional before signing the agreement.

Cafeteria

Employers can deduct the cost of a company cafeteria if more than 50% of the meals eaten there were for the employer's convenience.

Expense category: Varies depending on actual expenses.

Campaign Contributions

Not deductible. See **Political Contributions**.

Cancellation Penalties

Deductible.
Expense category: Other expenses.

Capital Assets

Capital assets are more commonly known as business assets, fixed assets, or depreciable assets. They include machinery, equipment, furniture, etc: assets that are used in the business.

Some capital assets can be deducted the year purchased, some must be depreciated over several years. See **Business Assets** and **Depreciation**.

Expense category: Depreciation. You must also fill out Form 4562, "Depreciation and Amortization."

Who Gets Welfare, Item #86: Last year, Disneyland received $300,000 in taxpayers' money from the Department of Energy to put on a bigger and brighter nightly fireworks show. Walt Disney Corp. reported profits of over $1 billion. —Reported by the Boston Globe

---

Carrying Charges

Carrying charges and interest are usually deductible. See **Interest**.
Expense category: Interest.

Cartons

Cartons, boxes, and other containers and packaging that are used to hold the goods you sell, are considered part of your inventory and must be included in cost-of-goods-sold. See **Inventory**. If, however, the cost of the containers or packaging are not significant or used only occasionally, most businesses write them off currently as shipping supplies or office supplies.

Expense category: Supplies.

People make a mistake when they pay their legislators good salaries, expect them to work full time, and then complain about all the government intervention in their lives. The nature of legislators is to legislate. They work full time introducing new bills that create more agencies, bureaus, commissions and regulatory functions of government.

—Former California Senator H.R. Richardson

Casualty Losses

Business losses from fire, storm or other casualty, or from theft, shoplifting or vandalism are fully deductible to the extent they are not covered by insurance.

Stolen or destroyed depreciable property (business assets that you are depreciating) can be deducted as a casualty loss, but only to the extent of the undepreciated balance. The portion you already depreciated was deducted as a depreciation expense in prior years, and cannot be deducted a second time. If you wrote the entire asset off the first year, you have no deductible loss.

Inventory that is stolen or destroyed should not be shown as a casualty loss. The inventory loss is deducted as part of your cost-of-goods-sold. See **Inventory**.

For more information, see IRS Publication 547, "Casualties, Disasters and Thefts."

Expense category: Depends on what kind of property is affected. You also must fill out Form 4684, "Casualties and Thefts."

Politics is about the redistribution of wealth, and I'm not talking about communism. Rich corporations distribute some wealth to campaigns. Consultants distribute that money to themselves and to highly skilled makers of crummy TV ads designed to keep people from voting. After the election, the politicians redistribute your income, generally in the direction of the people who gave it to them. It's what you might call a closed system. Closed to you, anyway.

—Rob Morse, San Francisco Chronicle

In the last national election, only 37.8% of the registered voters went to the polls.

—U.S.A. Today

Charitable Contributions

Only corporations can deduct charitable contributions and donations as a business deduction, and only if the charities have IRS charitable non-profit status. Corporations can deduct up to 10% of their taxable income. Contributions of $250 or more must be substantiated by a written acknowledgement or receipt from the recipient.

Corporations that donate used equipment, furniture or other depreciable assets cannot claim a deduction if the assets are already depreciated or written off.

C corporations (not S corporations) that donate inventory to qualified charities can get a deduction for more than the cost of the inventory. They can deduct the cost plus half the difference between cost and regular sales price, up to twice the cost of the inventory.

Corporations that donate computers to qualifying schools or public libraries can get a deduction for up to twice the basis of the property. (This deduction is scheduled to expire December 31, 2003).

Sole proprietorships, partnerships, and limited liability companies may not take deductions for charitable contributions. The owners of these businesses, however, may be able to deduct charitable contributions on their personal 1040 returns.

Expense category: Charitable contributions (corporations only).

Charitable contribution as promotion: In a recent IRS ruling, a business donated money to a charitable organization, and as a result got favorable publicity. The donation was not deductible as a charitable contribution, because it did not meet IRS requirements. But the donation was fully deductible as an advertising cost. This may be a way around deduction limitations on some charitable contributions. You should ask your accountant about this possible tax deduction.

Expense category: Advertising.

Chauffeur

As I discussed in the beginning of this book, all business expenses, in order to be deductible, must meet three IRS requirements. They must be (1) ordinary, (2) necessary, and (3) not lavish or extravagant. If you can look an underpaid, underappreciated IRS agent in the eye, and convince him that the cost of hiring your personal chauffeur is ordinary, necessary, and not lavish or extravagant, I congratulate you.

Expense category: Legal and professional services?

McDonald's Corp. ranked just above the Internal Revenue Service in a customer satisfaction survey performed for Fortune magazine, and the IRS was dead last.
—Reported in the San Francisco Chronicle, Business Section

Child Care

Some child care expenses are deductible, some are not. See **Dependent Care**.

Child Care Business: Expenses for running a child care business are deductible like the expenses of any other business. If you run a child care business out of your home, see **Home Office** for special child care deductions allowed.

The Federal Market Promotion Program has handed $1.2 billion of your tax dollars to trade associations which then hand your tax dollars to well-heeled corporations, agribusinesses and alcohol giants. Gallo received $4.3 million of your tax dollars. $10 million went to Sunkist, with annual sales of some $1 billion. Pillsbury received $2.9 million. McDonald's got $465,000 to promote Chicken McNuggets abroad. Supporters argue that these companies need your money to compete against foreign corporations. You see, poor little McDonald's, with annual revenues of $7 billion, can't compete without your dough. Members of Congress take your money and give it to somebody else, little guys like McDonald's and Gallo.

—Syndicated columnist Debra J. Saunders

Children on Payroll

You can hire your children, get a deduction for their wages, and—within certain limitations—the children are not subject to income or payroll taxes.

The rules are very specific, but generally, if your child is under eighteen, has absolutely no "unearned income" such as bank interest, and does legitimate work for your business, you can pay your child up to $4,700 a year tax free and get a business deduction for the wages (2002 maximum; amount increases almost every year). The child does not have to file a federal income tax return, and owes no federal income taxes. And you, the parent-employer get a full tax deduction for the wages paid. It's a rare tax law indeed that lets you have your cake and eat it too.

If the child does have unearned income such as bank interest, or if the child is earning more than $4,700 a year (2002), the child must file an income tax return. But the child's wages, regardless of the amount paid, are exempt from federal payroll taxes (Social Security and Medicare taxes).

This rule applies only to sole proprietorships and husband-and-wife partnerships, and it has a lot of variables. For more information, see IRS Publication 15, "Circular E, Employer's Tax Guide."

Also check with your state employment department before you hire your children. Many states have laws similar to the IRS, and impose no state income or payroll taxes, nor require worker's compensation insurance on your children. Check your state employer's guide. Do not rely on verbal information from state agencies. People who work at state employment departments are often unaware of child employment laws.

Children who hire their parents get no special tax breaks. The parents are considered regular employees, subject to all regular employment and income taxes.

Expense category: Wages.

Classes

Some classes are deductible. See **Education**.

Expense category: Other expenses.

Cleaning Service

Cleaning and janitorial services for the business premises are deductible. Cleaning and laundry services for clothing used exclusively for work are deductible, but only if the clothing is unsuitable for street wear, such as a uniform, costume, or protective gear.

Cleaning and laundry services for your regular clothing are deductible when travelling away from home overnight on business.

Expense category: Office expense. Travel (if travelling).

It has become popular to call the Tax Code "the IRS Code", suggesting that the IRS is responsible for it. The IRS didn't write it, Congress did. Congress is responsible for the tax mess. Republicans and Democrats alike. After three years of GOP rule, the tax code is in the same sad shape it was after decades of fiddling by Congresses run mostly by Democrats.

—Kiplinger Tax Report, Washington, D.C.

Closing Costs

Loan closing costs can include broker commission, processing fees, title insurance, property taxes, termite reports, transfer taxes, loan fees, points, and other costs. Some of these closing costs are deductible immediately, some must be deducted over a period of years. This is a complicated area of law that may need the help of a tax accountant. See **Loans. Interest. Property Taxes**.

Expense category: Varies depending on actual expenses.

Clothing

Clothing used exclusively for work and unsuitable for street wear is deductible. Includes uniforms, costumes, and protective gear. Cost of cleaning is also deductible.

Clothing with your company's logo or advertising is considered a uniform, and therefore deductible.

Expense category: Supplies.

Tax Court memo 1998-283: A salesman refused to pay the self-employment [Social Security] tax because of Social Security's impending insolvency. Tax Court ruled that, "Expecting zero doesn't excuse not paying."

Clubs

Dues and other expenses for business groups, professional organizations, merchant and trade associations, chambers of commerce, etc. are deductible. Dues to community service organizations, such as Rotary, Lions, etc., are also deductible.

Expense category: Other expenses.

If part of your dues to a trade or professional association are for political lobbying, that portion of the dues is not deductible.

Dues and membership fees in clubs run for pleasure, recreation, or other social purposes are not deductible. These include athletic, luncheon, hotel, airline, sporting and other entertainment or recreational organizations, associations, clubs and facilities. Even if you use a club membership solely to generate or discuss business, the dues are not deductible. Sometimes the term "business club" is used to describe such a facility. If the "business" club is not a business organization, the dues are not deductible. Entertainment costs at these clubs, if for business, are 50% deductible. See **Entertainment**.

Coffee Service

Deductible. Deductible. Deductible. Thank you.
Expense category: Office expense.

It's difficult to make your friends believe you make as much as you do and have the government believe you make as little as you do.
—Sam Leandro, professional musician

Commissions

Commissions paid to outside salespeople or companies, commissions paid for referrals, finders fees, and the like are deductible.
Expense category: Commissions and fees.

Commissions paid to acquire new customers who sign long term contracts, may have to be capitalized, and deducted over a period of years. The IRS says the deduction must be spread over the average number of years new customers stay with the business. This is something you should ask your accountant about.

Real estate commissions must be added to the cost of the real estate and depreciated. See **Depreciation**.

A business broker's commission for helping to buy or sell a business may have to be amortized (deducted) over five years. See **Buying a Business.**
Expense category: Depreciation. You must also fill out Form 4562, "Depreciation and Amortization."

Community Service

Community service expenses are often deductible, depending on what you actually are spending money on. You should check with your accountant.

Expense category: Varies depending on actual expenses.

Commuting

Regular commuting expenses, home to your regular place of business and back, are not deductible. Side trips to customers or to suppliers are deductible. See **Vehicles**.

Home-Based Businesses: Since your home is your regular place of business, you have no commuting expenses. All business travel is fully deductible. See **Vehicles**.

Employers: Employers can pay up to $65 a month per employee for transit passes or employer-provided van pool vehicles, and the payments are not taxable to the employees.

Expense category: Employee benefit programs.

The IRS encourages people to round off numbers. For example, my income is $34,500, so I round this off to $30,000.
    —John Soennichsen-Cheney, First Runner Up, Dave Barry's Amateur Tax Tips Contest, Home Office Computing Magazine

---

Compensation

Compensation to employees is deductible. Compensation paid to independent contractors and commissioned salespeople is deductible. Compensation to yourself is deductible only if you are an employee of your own corporation. See: **Payroll. Commissions. Draw.**

Expense category: Wages. (for employees). Commissions and fees (for independent contractors, salespeople, other non-employees).

I.R.S. Service Center, Ogden, Utah

Computers

Computers can be deducted or depreciated. See **Business Assets** and **Depreciation**. If the computer is used away from your business premises, the computer must be used more than 50% for business, or no deduction allowed.

Expense category: Depreciation. You must also fill out Form 4562, "Depreciation and Amortization."

Computer Programs

See **Software**.

Whatever the revenue may be, there will always be the pressing need to spend it.

—*Parkinson's Second Law, Prof. C. Northcote Parkinson*

Condominium

Business condominiums that you lease are deductible.
Expense category: Rent or lease.

Business condominiums that you own must be depreciated like any other business building. See **Depreciation.**

Condominium Associations, Management Fees, Etc. are deductible if business related.
Expense category: Legal and professional services.

Home-Based Businesses: You can deduct a percentage of your condominium lease, or depreciate a percentage of your condo if you own it, and deduct a percentage of any related fees, but only if you are allowed a home office deduction. See **Home Office**. Home-office depreciation is reported on Form 8829, "Expenses for Business Use of Your Home."

Conferences

Costs of conducting or attending business conferences are deductible. Travel (with a few exceptions) and lodging are deductible. Meals are 50% deductible. See Travel. Meals.

Expense category: Other expenses (for the conference itself). Travel.

If you want to know how anyone can stop paying taxes, the answer seems to be: the same way porcupines make love. Very, very gingerly.
—Samuel Thesham, Accountant of the Wild West

Consignment

Consigned inventory is merchandise a business or self-employed individual places with another business for the other business to try to sell.

For example, a dress maker may consign inventory to a dress shop. The business consigning the goods (the dress maker) has not made a sale and does not get paid until the business that has taken the goods in on consignment (the dress shop) sells the goods.

For tax and inventory purposes, the consignor (in our example, the dress maker) has not sold the dress. There is no income to report. The dress should be included in the dress maker's year-end inventory. The consignee (the dress shop) has not purchased the dress until it re-sells the dress to its customer. The dress shop does not include the dress in its year-end inventory.

Consignors should be warned that these consignment laws are income tax laws only. They may not hold up in bankruptcy court. If the dress shop files for bankruptcy before it sells the dress, the court can seize and sell consigned inventory to pay off the creditors of the dress shop, even though the shop doesn't legally own the goods. The dress maker will have to stand in line with all the other creditors hoping to get paid.

The dress maker can protect him or herself by filing what's known as a UCC 1 (for Uniform Commercial Code) form with the county or state where the dress shop is located. This is a legal notice that the goods belong to the dress maker and not to the dress shop. It will usually hold up in bankruptcy court, enabling the consignor to get the unsold merchandise back.

If the dress was sold by the dress shop, but the shop filed for bankruptcy before paying the dress maker, the courts hold that this was a sale, that the dress maker is just another creditor who probably will never see her money. A UCC 1 filing will not help.

See **Inventory**.

Expense category: Cost of goods sold.

Construction

Building or other major construction must be depreciated. See **Depreciation**.

Expense category: Depreciation. You must also fill out Form 4562, "Depreciation and Amortization."

The blame for the maddening complications of the federal tax system goes to the people with the most money. They put the complexity into the tax laws to get out of paying, and now they cry out against the side effects of the imbecilities wrought by their own lobbyists. They denounce the inconveniences attendant on the very favors they bought themselves with their campaign contributions. Talk about wanting it both ways.

—Columnist Nicholas Von Hoffman

Consultants

Definition of a consultant: Someone who borrows your watch to tell you what time it is.

Definition of a consultant: Someone who saves his client almost enough money to pay his fee.

Consultants' fees are deductible.

Expense category: Commissions and fees.

Containers

Boxes, cartons, and other containers and packaging materials that hold the goods you sell, are considered part of your inventory and must be included in cost-of-goods-sold. See **Inventory**. If, however, the cost of the containers or packaging is not significant or used only occasionally, most businesses deduct them as a current expense.

Expense category: Supplies.

Butterfat, the key ingredient in ice cream, cheese, and butter, is in short supply, and prices have surged 73% this year. Why the pinch? The federal government subsidized the export of 40 million pounds of butter over the past year. —Reported in Business Week Magazine

---

Contamination Cleanup

Cost of cleaning up contamination caused by your own business is deductible.

Expense category: Repairs and maintenance.

Cost of cleaning up contamination created by a prior landowner must be capitalized. No current deduction, except for certain federally qualified contamination sites.

Contractors

Building contractors' fees and subcontractors' fees may have to be added to the cost of the building, and depreciated. See **Depreciation**. Minor work and repairs can be deducted.

Expense category: Repairs and maintenance; or Depreciation (you must also fill out Form 4562, "Depreciation and Amortization").

Also see **Independent Contractors**.

Contracts

The cost of preparing contracts is deductible. A payment to be released from a contract is deductible.

Expense category: Legal and professional services.

Contracts that are expensive to negotiate and prepare, and cover more than a year, must be amortized over the length of the contract.
Expense category: Depreciation. You must also fill out Form 4562, "Depreciation and Amortization."

Contributions

Money you contribute to your own business is neither income nor expense, and is not deductible.

Also see **Charitable Contributions** and **Political Contributions**.

Conventions

The cost of attending a business convention in the United States is deductible. Travel and lodging expenses are also deductible, meals are 50% deductible, entertainment is 50% deductible. The expense of a spouse travelling with you is not deductible unless the spouse is a partner or employee in the business and has a valid business reason for attending. Conventions overseas may also be deductible, although the IRS has stricter rules. See **Travel**.

Expense category: Travel.

Copyrights

Copyrights and many other intangible assets must be amortized (deducted) over a period of years. Copyrights are so inexpensive, however, that I would suggest that if you only have one or a few, write them off anyway. For more information on writing off assets over a period of years, see **Depreciation**.

Expense category: Taxes and licenses; or Depreciation (if you depreciate copyrights, you must also fill out Form 4562, "Depreciation and Amortization").

The income tax is losing the confidence of the American people. Make no mistake about that. —Former Senator William V. Roth

---

Cost of Goods Sold

Businesses cannot deduct the cost of inventory until the goods are sold. The expense is called "cost-of-goods-sold." See **Inventory.**
Expense category: Cost of goods sold.

Costumes

Clothing used exclusively for work and unsuitable for street wear is deductible. This also includes uniforms and protective gear. Cost of cleaning is also deductible.
Expense category: Supplies.

Who Gets Welfare, Item #333: Military contractor Lockheed Martin received $850 million of taxpayers' money from the Pentagon to pay the cost of the merger of Lockheed and Martin Marietta. The Pentagon paid an additional $100 million of taxpayers' money to top executives of Lockheed and Martin Marietta as a bonus for successfully completing the merger. That amount included $20,000 for golf balls.
—Reported by the Boston Globe

Courier Service

Any business service of this type is deductible.
Expense category: Office expense.

Credit Cards

Business purchases made with a credit card are fully deductible. Fees and interest are also fully deductible. You can use your personal credit card for business purchases. You get a full business deduction for business purchases. If the card is used partly for business, you must prorate any bank charges or credit card fees, personal vs. business. And, only the interest on business purchases can be deducted.
Expense category: Office expense (for bank fees). Interest (for interest charges).

Corporations: If you are an employee of your own corporation, and if you use your personal credit card to pay corporate bills, have the corporation reimburse you for your employee business expenses, to get the best tax advantage. See **Employee Business Expenses**.

Credits

See **Tax Credits**.

Customs

Customs fees, duties and tariffs are deductible. Fees charged by customs brokers and international handlers are deductible. Instead of deducting customs fees immediately, in some cases the fees and duties can be added to the cost of inventory and written off as cost of goods sold. You may want to ask your accountant about this.

Expense category: Commissions and fees. Taxes and licenses.

Too bad all the people who know how to run the country are busy driving taxicabs and cutting hair.
— George Burns

Damaged Property

If business assets are damaged or destroyed, you are entitled to a deduction. See **Casualty Losses**.

Damages

Penalties for breach of contract are sometimes called damages. They are deductible.

Expense category: Other expenses.

Damage to business property is deductible. See **Casualty Losses**.
Damaged inventory is deductible as part of cost-of-goods-sold. See **Inventory**.

Day Care

Some day care expenses are deductible. See **Dependent Care**.

Day Care Business: Expenses for running a day care business are deductible like the expenses of any other business. If you run a day care business out of your home, see **Home Office** for special day care deductions allowed.

Decorating

Decorating expenses are deductible.
Expense category: Office expense.

Valuable art treasures and antiques cannot be written off until sold. See **Art Treasures**.

Delivery Charges

If you pay delivery charges on goods you sell, the expenses are fully deductible.

Delivery charges on goods you receive are deductible, with two exceptions: Freight charges for inventory you are buying must be included as part of the cost of the inventory. See **Inventory**. Freight charges for business assets you are buying (machinery, furniture, etc.) should be added to the cost of the asset. See **Business Assets**. However, if the amounts are minor, most businesses just deduct the delivery charges when paid.

Expense category: Other expenses.

Business people often underestimate the number of able, conscientious and zealous people working for government in Washington—and Albany, Springfield, and Sacramento. They're usually overworked and underpaid. And motivated primarily by pride and faith in what they're doing. Try treating them that way. Walk in and say, "You're my government, help me." And they will, and love you for asking. It's a refreshing change for them.
—Robert Townsend from Up the Organization

Demolition

The cost to demolish a building must be added to the cost basis of the land. It cannot be deducted.

Cost of removing storage tanks is deductible.

Expense category: Other expenses.

Dependent Care

Dependent care (child care, day care) provided for your employees' families is deductible. You can also pay employees money for them to spend on dependent care, tax-free to the employees (up to $5,000 per year). You the employer get a deduction.

Expense category: Employee benefit programs.

Dependent care for your own family is not deductible as a business expense unless you are incorporated. (You may, however, be eligible for a dependent care tax credit on your personal 1040 return).

Dependent Care Business: If you operate a dependent care (day care) business out of your home, there are special office-in-home rules just for day care businesses. See **Home Office**.

Politicians are making whoopee with the taxpayers' money. When the founding fathers guaranteed the right to pursue happiness, this is not what they meant. —Ron Crickenberger, Libertarian Party, denouncing taxpayer funding, through Medicaid, of Viagra, Pfizer's pill for male impotence.

Make love, not war. —Country Joe and the Fish, 1968

Depletion

If you own mineral property or standing timber, you can take a deduction for depletion. check with your accountant.

Expense category: Depletion.

Deposits

Refundable deposits are not deductible. Non-refundable deposits are deductible. Deposits that are actually prepayments of some expense come under the prepaid expense rules. See **Prepayments.**

Some deposits are called advances. An advance is really a prepayment for work to be done or goods to be delivered, not money you expect to get back. Advances are deductible. See **Advances.**

Expense category: Varies depending on actual expenses.

According to the Internal Revenue Service, the number 1040 (Form 1040) was a random selection. In Old England, Lady Godiva rode naked through the streets of Coventry to protest oppressive taxes. The year was 1040.

Depreciation

Depreciation is a tax term and means that the tax deduction for an asset is spread out over several years. When you depreciate an asset, you do not deduct the entire cost of the asset the year you purchase it. Each year, a portion of the cost is deducted. These assets are variously called fixed, capital, depreciable, or business assets.

Depreciable assets include buildings, vehicles, machinery, shop and office equipment, fixtures, tools, aircraft, boats, trailers, intangibles such as trademarks, patents and software, some farm animals, plants and trees. Major building improvements such as a new roof, and major repairs that extend the life of an asset, must be treated as depreciable assets. Both new and used assets can be depreciated.

Depreciable assets do not include inventory, supplies, inexpensive tools or anything that will not last more than a year.

The IRS has several depreciation methods you must choose from, and several different "write off periods" or "recovery periods"—how many years you must write off different assets. There are several categories of assets, each with a different write off period. The categories most used by small businesses are:

3 Year Property: on-road tractor units, race horses over two years old, all horses over 12 years old, software, web site design.

5 Year Property: vehicles; trailers; aircraft; most equipment used for research and experimentation; computers, copiers, fax machines, and similar office equipment; carpeting; movable partitions; semi-conductor manufacturing equipment; solar, wind and some other alternative energy property; some electronic equipment; appliances, furniture and rugs used in residential rental property.

7 Year Property: most machinery, equipment, furniture, fixtures, most signs (except large outdoor signs, which are 15 year property); railroad track; horses other than those listed as 3-year Property.

10 Year Property: most boats (except pleasure craft, which are not deductible); barges and tugs; single-purpose agricultural and horticultural structures; fruit and nut trees and vines.

15 Year Property: gas stations, including their mini-marts (with some exceptions). Some golf course improvements. Large outdoor signs. Some intangible (intellectual) property such as goodwill, trademarks, trade names, franchises, customer lists, and covenants not to compete. Patents and copyrights are 15 year property only if acquired as part of a business you have purchased.

20 Year Property: all-purpose farm buildings.

27½ Year Property: residential rental buildings.

39 Year Property: all buildings other than residential rental property, farm buildings, and some gas stations.

Other: Patents and copyrights must be depreciated over the life granted by the government (except see 15 year property above).

IRS depreciation rules change almost every year. Whatever rule was in effect when you purchased an asset (or when you first used it in business if you purchased it before going into business) is the rule you must use for that asset for as long as you own the asset. So if you have been in business and buying depreciable assets for several years, you will be calculating depreciation using several different sets of rules! Depreciation can get quite complicated, and is one main reason businesses seek the help of tax accountants.

Assets owned before going into business: Depreciable assets used in your business that were purchased before going into business can be depreciated regardless of when acquired. These assets must be valued at their cost or at their market value at the time the assets are first used in your business, whichever is less. If some old machinery, or an old computer, which cost you $2,000 eight years ago, was only worth $500 (market value) when first used in your business, you may only depreciate $500.

Assets used partly for business: Depreciable assets used partly for business and partly for non-business can be depreciated to the extent used for business. For example, if you use your tools 50% for business and 50% for personal use, you can depreciate 50% of the cost.

First Year Write-Off option: For most depreciable assets (other than buildings and intangibles), depreciation is not a requirement, it is an option. At your option, up to $24,000 of depreciable assets can be deducted, instead of being depreciated, the year of purchase. Any assets in excess of the $24,000 maximum must be depreciated. (2002 maximum). For full details, see **Business Assets**. Buildings (with some exceptions) and intangibles are not eligible for the deduction. They must be depreciated.

The First Year Write-Off is very easy to calculate, and depreciation is very difficult to calculate. So, why would anyone choose complex, multi-year depreciation over the simple, write-it-off-now deduction? Many new businesses make little or no profit the first year or two, and may not have any use for the additional tax savings the First Year Write-Off deduction offers. It might be better to depreciate the assets, spreading the deduction over several years. In this way, you deduct the bulk of the expense in future years when you can use it to save taxes. You might want to calculate your profit and taxes under both methods to find the bigger tax savings.

Limitations on Automobiles: Regardless of the percent used for business or the depreciation method used, automobile depreciation (and the Sec. 179 deduction) is limited to a maximum of $3,060 the first year, $4,900 the second year, $2,950 the third year, and $,1775 each succeeding year (2001 amounts. Dollar limits change from year to year. Check with the IRS). Due to this limitation, expensive cars cannot be fully depreciated in the five years normally allowed. Depreciation is spread out over a longer period. This limitation is for automobiles only, not for trucks, vans, large SUVs or any other vehicles with a Gross Weight over 6,000 pounds.

For full depreciation details, see IRS Publication 946, "How to Depreciate Property."
Expense category: Depreciation. You must also fill out Form 4562, "Depreciation and Amortization."

Design Costs

Minor, routine and on-going design costs are deductible.

Graphic and package design costs are also deductible, according to the Tax Court. The IRS disagrees. If there is substantial money involved, you should ask your accountant about this.
Expense category: Advertising.

Large design costs that will benefit future years may have to be amortized (deducted) over several years. You should ask your accountant about this.
Expense category: Depreciation. You must also fill out Form 4562, "Depreciation and Amortization."

I'm not a grouch the whole month.
—Unidentified San Francisco coffee retailer, on April 15, interviewed in Inc. Magazine.

Development

Product development expenses are usually deductible, and may also be eligible for special tax credits (see **Tax Credits**).

Some development expenses that will benefit future years may have to be capitalized, and deducted over a period of at least five years. You should discuss these expenses with your accountant.

Expense category: Other expenses.

Business development expenses may or may not be deductible, depending on whether you are just starting your business or already have an operating business. **See Start-Up Costs.**

Real estate developers: Pre-development costs such as planning and design, blueprints, building permits, engineering studies, landscape plans, and the like, cannot be deducted currently, but must be capitalized. See **Buildings, Land, Renovations, Property Taxes, Restoration**.

Directors' Fees

Fees paid to corporate directors are deductible.

Expense category: Commissions and fees.

Disability Insurance

Disability insurance for your employees is deductible. Disability insurance for yourself is not deductible unless you are an employee of your corporation. Insurance that pays for business overhead expenses during a time you are disabled is deductible.

Expense category: Employee benefit programs (for employees); Insurance (for Overhead Insurance).

Disaster Losses

Deductible, but with special rules. See **Casualty Losses**.

How can small businesses be so successful in the United States when our government appears so unfriendly and unhelpful?

—Former Senator Bob Dole

Discounts

"List price $1,599.00. On Sale today only $14.95." Discounts given to customers and employees reduce your income. You show a lower gross income (sales) on your tax return. Discounts are not shown as an expense deduction.

You can give discounts to employees and their families for anything your business makes or sells, tax-free to them, as long as the discounted price is not below your cost.

Discounts on purchases reduce the cost of the items being purchased. Discounts should not be recorded or deducted separately.

Displays

Goods on display are considered inventory. See **Inventory**.
Display fixtures are business assets. See **Business Assets**.
Display decorations can be deducted.
Expense Category: Supplies.

Joseph Nunan occupies a unique place in the history of the Internal Revenue Service. Nunan, who was IRS commissioner from 1944 through 1947, was convicted in 1952 on five counts of income tax evasion.
—Reported by the Associated Press

Dividends

When corporations distribute their profits to shareholders, these distributions are called dividends. These dividends are not considered business expenses and are not deductible. Any costs associated with distributing dividends, such as bank or broker fees, are deductible.

For regular C corporations, dividends paid to shareholders are taxed twice: The corporation pays corporate income tax on the profits earned. And the shareholders of the corporation pay personal income tax on those same profits when the profits are distributed as dividends. Double taxation.

To avoid the double taxation, many small corporations (whose shareholders are also employees) pay as much of their income as possible to the owner-employees as salaries and year-end bonuses. Sometime in December, the corporation figures out how much of a profit the business will probably make, and then gives out (or doesn't give out) year-end bonuses to get those profits down to zero.

Unlike dividends, the salaries and bonuses are deductible to the corporation, thus reducing its taxes. The shareholder-employees pay personal income taxes on their salaries and year-end bonuses, the same income tax they'd pay if they got dividends. But the profits are taxed only once, to the shareholders. As long as the combined wages and bonuses are "reasonable" (comparable to what executives in similar companies earn), the IRS is not likely to challenge the arrangement. Paying salaries instead of dividends, however, increases payroll taxes on the corporation and on the owner-employee, sometimes substantially. But the additional payroll taxes are usually much less than the double income taxes resulting from dividends.

Here is a warning: Corporations that pay out most of their profits in salaries *or* in dividends should be careful they don't drain the business of too much cash, leaving the company "undercapitalized": not enough money to run the business or pay the creditors. Should this happen, the courts can throw out the limited liability protection (called "piercing the corporate veil") and hold the owners personally liable for corporate debts.

The above discussion applies only to C corporations, not to S corporations or Limited Liability Companies, neither of which pay income taxes. All of their earnings pass through to the owners, who pay personal income taxes on the business earnings.

Then came the churches, Then came the schools,
Then came the lawyers, Then came the rules.
                                   —Mark Knopfler, "Telegraph Road" (Dire Straits)

Dividend Rebates

The word dividend has a second meaning unrelated to corporate profits. Rebates to customers are sometimes called dividends. These rebates are deductible.

Expense category: Returns and allowances.

Donations

Only corporations can deduct charitable contributions and donations, although some businesses have been able to deduct charitable donations as advertising expenses. For more information, see **Charitable Contributions**.

Expense category: Charitable contributions.

Political donations are not deductible.

Gifts come under different tax laws. See **Business Gifts**.

The best thing Congress can do is go home for a couple of years.
—Will Rogers

Draw

Draw, partner, refers to drawing money out of your business. When you are self-employed, as a sole proprietor, partner in a partnership, or member (owner) of a limited liability company, you are not an employee of your business. You do not get a salary or a wage. If you want some money from your business, you "draw" it; that is, you just take it. This is not an expense, this is not a tax deduction. It is not a taxable transaction. See **Paying Yourself**.

Corporations: If you own a corporation, the rules are very different. You do not "draw" money, but you do pay yourself a salary, taxable as regular employee wages. Any money you take out of a corporation in excess of your salary is also not a draw. It is a dividend, also taxable. See **Payroll, Dividends**.

Drilling

The costs of drilling a well are deductible.
Expense category: Other expenses.

Driveways

You can deduct the costs of maintaining a private road or driveway on your business property.

Expense category: Repairs and maintenance; or Depreciation (you must also fill out Form 4562, "Depreciation and Amortization.")

The construction of a driveway must be depreciated. See **Depreciation**.

Expense category: Depreciation. You must also fill out Form 4562, "Depreciation and Amortization."

Virgil, of Old Rome, poet and author of the Aeneid, owned a Roman villa with land. Thereon, it is recorded, he buried a housefly after an elaborate funeral with pallbearers and eulogies. The ceremony qualified Virgil's land as a tax-free cemetery.

—Reported by E.M. Boyd, The Grab Bag
(with thanks to Sharon Kamoroff)

Dues

Dues for business groups, professional organizations, merchant and trade associations, chambers of commerce, etc. are deductible. Dues to community service organizations, such as Rotary, Lions, etc., are also deductible.

Expense category: Other expenses.

If part of your dues to a trade or professional association are for political lobbying, that portion of the dues is not deductible.

Dues and membership fees in clubs run for pleasure, recreation, or other social purposes are not deductible. These include athletic, luncheon, hotel, airline, sporting and other entertainment or recreational organizations, associations, clubs and facilities. Even if you use a club membership solely to generate or discuss business, the dues are not deductible. Sometimes the term "business club" is used to describe such a facility. If the "business" club is not a business organization, the dues are not deductible.

Duties

Customs fees, duties, and tariffs are deductible. Fees charged by customs brokers and international handlers are deductible. Instead of deducting customs duties immediately, in some cases the duties can be added to the cost of inventory and written off as cost-of-goods-sold. You may want to ask your accountant about this.

Expense category: Legal and professional services. Taxes and licenses.

There is no such thing as a simple answer to a complex problem if you wish to be fair. But if any solution becomes too complex, voluntary compliance becomes impossible.

—Vern Hoven, Vern Hoven Tax Seminars

Education Expenses

Self Employed Education Deduction:

The cost of education for any self-employed individual is deductible, but only if the education maintains or improves a skill required in your business. Education expenses are not allowed if the education is required to meet minimum educational requirements of your present business or if the education will qualify you for a new trade or business.

A self-employed welder who takes a course in a new welding method can charge the expense to the business. A self-employed dance teacher who also takes dance lessons can deduct the cost of the lessons. On the other hand, a leather craftsperson who takes a woodworking course cannot deduct the expenses. The education must be directly related to the business you already operate. Taking a course in pottery *before* opening your pottery shop is not deductible. Any self- employed person can take a course in bookkeeping or taxes or computers and deduct the cost.

Education expenses include tuition, course fees, books, laboratory fees, travel between your business and the class location, and travel expenses while away from home overnight. Overnight travel is subject to limitations. See **Travel**.

Expense category: Other expenses.

Employer Paid Education for Employees:
Employers can deduct, and employees can exclude from their income, the cost of job-related education expenses.

Employers can also pay up to $5,250 annually for employee education expenses that are not job related. Employer-paid employee education expenses in excess of $5,250 (if not job related) are considered taxable wages, treated as you would treat regular wages. Also see **Scholarships**.

Expense category: Employee benefit programs; Wages.

Do not confuse the two different deductions. The self-employed education deduction is for sole proprietors, partners, and members of limited liability companies. The employee education deduction is for employers only. If you are an employee of your own corporation, you would be eligible for the employer deduction, not the self employment deduction. If this does not make sense to you, it is explained further under **Draw** and **Paying Yourself**.

For more information, see IRS Publ. 508, "Education Expenses."

There is a universal reluctance to voluntarily pay taxes.
—Society of California Accountants

Electricity

Electricity and other utilities are deductible.
Expense category: Utilities.

Home-Based Businesses: You can deduct a percentage of your home utilities only if you are allowed a home office deduction. See **Home Office**. Home-office utilities are reported on Form 8829, "Expenses for Business Use of Your Home."

Manufacturers: Electricity for the manufacturing process may have to be added to the cost of the inventory rather than being written off immediately. See **Inventory**.

Employee Business Expenses

If the employer reimburses an employee for out-of-pocket business expenses, the employer is entitled to a tax deduction for the expenses. The reimbursement is not part of the employee's wages, is not subject to payroll taxes, and is not included on the employee's W-2 wage statement.

If the employer's reimbursement exceeds the employee's actual expenses, the excess is considered additional wages, deductible as payroll, and subject to payroll taxes.

If the employee does not receive a reimbursement or receives a reimbursement less than the actual expenses, the employee can take a partial (not full) itemized deduction on his or her 1040 tax return.

It is important to understand that the employer can get a full tax deduction by reimbursing the employee. The employee, if not reimbursed, cannot get a full tax deduction. Also remember that a self-employed individual—sole proprietor, partner, or owner of a limited liability company—is not an employee of the business. Employee business expense reimbursements do not apply to self-employed individuals. Owners of corporations *are* employees of their businesses.

Expense category: Varies depending on actual expenses.

Employees

Wages and benefits you pay your employees are deductible. See **Payroll** and **Fringe Benefits**. If you employ your spouse, see **Spouse**. If you employ your children, see **Children**.

Expense category: Wages.

Employment Agencies

Employment agency fees are deductible.

Expense category: Commissions and fees.

Employment Taxes

Deductible. See **Payroll Taxes**.

Expense category: Taxes and licenses.

"Don't you dare deduct *me*."

Entertainment

Only 50% of entertainment expenses are deductible.

In some cases there is a fine line as to what is entertainment (subject to the 50% limit) and what is not entertainment and therefore fully deductible. For example, a fashion show put on by a dress designer would not be considered entertainment, but a 100% deductible business expense. A party or lunch after the show, however, would be entertainment subject to the 50% limit.

Sometimes the term "promotion" is also called "entertainment." But promotion expenses are fully deductible, and entertainment is limited to a 50% deduction. You get to define your own expenses: the right choice of words will get you the right deduction. Entertainment is more likely to get an IRS second look than other expenses. So don't classify an expense as entertainment unless it truly is.

A company or holiday party where all employees are invited (as well as customers and prospective customers) is 100% deductible.

The cost of owning or leasing an entertainment facility is not deductible. Travel to and from an entertainment event or facility, including parking, is 100% deductible.

For more information, see IRS Publ. 463, "Travel, Entertainment and Gift Expenses."

Expense category: Travel, meals and entertainment.

Environmental Remediation

See **Contamination Cleanup**.

Equipment

Equipment can be deducted or depreciated. See **Business Assets**.

Expense category: Depreciation. You must also fill out Form 4562, "Depreciation and Amortization."

In a recent study in Economic Inquiry, researchers found that 69 million taxpayers claiming refunds on their federal taxes lost nearly $1 billion in interest their money could have earned if they had filed at the end of January. More than a third waited until April or later to send in their returns. People clearly abhor the task of tax preparation and put it off as long as possible, even if they are owed a refund.

—Reported in Business Week

Estimated Taxes

Owners of unincorporated businesses and self-employed individuals are required to make quarterly prepayments of their federal income and self-employment taxes, if the combined taxes are $1,000 or more. The government wants your tax money, in advance, just like the taxes withheld from employee paychecks. Use Form 1040-ES.

Corporations must make quarterly tax prepayments if estimated federal income tax for the year is $500 or more. File Form 8109.

These estimated tax payments are not deductible expenses.

Exchange

Exchange, as in trade or barter, is a taxable transaction. Goods and services received in trade are deductible just like goods and services purchased with cash. See **Barter**.

Expense category: Varies depending on actual expenses.

Of the ten million people who unlawfully do not file tax returns, 3.5 million were due refunds.

—Reported in the New York Times

Excise Taxes

Federal excise taxes, if levied, are deductible.

More information: see IRS Publication 510, "Excise Taxes."

Some states call their corporate income tax an excise tax. It is deductible on your federal return.

Expense category: Taxes and licenses.

Expense Accounts

Deductible, depending on what the expenses are actually for. See **Employee Business Expenses**.

Exporting

Customs fees, duties and tariffs are deductible. Fees charged by customs brokers and international handlers are deductible.

Expense category: Commissions and fees. Taxes and licenses.

Exterminator Service

Deductible.

Expense category: Office expense; or Other Expenses.

Family

A spouse or a parent on your payroll are treated like any other employee, except a spouse and parents are not subject to Federal Unemployment (FUTA) tax. (Unincorporated businesses only). See **Spouse. Parents on Payroll.**

Your own children on the payroll, if under the age of eighteen, may be exempt from income and payroll taxes. See **Children**.
Expense category: Wages.

Honey, from what I can see of your accounting skills, the country would be better served if you were dishing up chicken fried steak on some Interstate in West Texas.

—Carole Ward, to IRS auditor Paula Dzierzanowski, during an audit of Ms. Ward's tax return. The result of the audit and the insult: armed IRS agents raided Ms. Ward's business and posted signs on her padlocked doors intimating that she was a drug smuggler. Ms. Ward subsequently sued the IRS and was awarded $325,000 in damages. (Nolo Law News).

FICA Tax

FICA stands for Federal Insurance Contributions Act. FICA tax is another name for the combined Medicare and Social Security payroll taxes deducted from every employee's paycheck and collected from every employer. Employer's portion is deductible. See **Social Security Tax**.
Expense category: Taxes and licenses.

Finance Charges

Finance charges are usually deductible. But see **Interest**.
Expense category: Interest.

Finders Fees

Finders fees, commissions, and the like, are deductible.
Expense category: Commissions and fees.

Ralph Kramden, reading from an IRS notice: "Failure to pay any estimated tax or taxes, or to file a return other than a return required under Section 13.03 or 13.04 hereunder, or to file a Notice of Exemption therefrom pursuant to Regulation 98.68(g) promulgated hereunder..."

Ed Norton: "Boy, Ralph, it sounds like you're in trouble."

Ralph: "Trouble? I don't even know what I'm talking about."
—The Honeymooners

Fines

Fines and penalties for violation of the law are not deductible. Penalties for not meeting contract requirements, and any other fines or penalties that do not involve breaking the law, are deductible.

Expense category: Other expenses.

Fire Protection Systems

Simple fire protection equipment such as a fire extinguisher can be deducted.

More elaborate systems must be treated like other business assets. See **Business Assets**. If the system is an integral part of a building, it must be depreciated along with the building. See **Depreciation**.

Expense category: Office expense; or Depreciation (you must also fill out Form 4562, "Depreciation and Amortization").

First Aid

Medical supplies, emergency supplies, aspirin, etc. are fully deductible.

Expense category: Office expense.

Fixed Assets

Fixed assets are machinery, equipment, furniture, and the like, assets the business owns, not for sale. They're staying, or fixed, as in fixed in place, not as in fixed a million times and they still don't work.

Fixed assets are also known as capital assets, depreciable assets, and business assets. Some fixed assets are deductible the year purchased, and some must be depreciated. See **Business Assets** and **Depreciation.**

Expense category: Depreciation. You must also fill out Form 4562, "Depreciation and Amortization."

There is a big gap between what the IRS permits and what companies do in practice.

—Nation's Business, U.S. Chamber of Commerce

Fixed Costs

Fixed costs refer to overhead, the dozens of large and small expenses you must pay whether you are generating income or not. Most fixed costs are deductible. See **Overhead.**

Expense category: Varies depending on actual expenses.

Fixing Up Expenses

Minor repairs and remodeling expenses are deductible. Major repairs and renovation will have to be added to the cost of the building and depreciated. See **Depreciation.**

Expense category: Repairs and maintenance; or Depreciation (you must also fill out Form 4562, "Depreciation and Amortization").

Fixtures

Shop and building fixtures, if not an integral part of the structure, can be deducted the year of purchase or depreciated. See **Business Assets.** Expensive fixtures that become a permanent part of a building must be added to the cost of the building and depreciated. See **Depreciation.**

Expense category: Depreciation. You must also fill out Form 4562, "Depreciation and Amortization."

Floor Tax

This is actually a property tax on inventory, sometimes levied by local and state governments. Inventory sits on the floor, that is why the tax is sometimes called a floor tax. Inventory also sits on shelves, but the tax is never called a shelf tax. Whatever it is or isn't called, the tax is deductible.

Expense category: Taxes and licenses.

The IRS has squandered nearly $4 billion during the past decade to bring its vast computer system up to date, but the new computers don't work.
—San Francisco Chronicle

Maybe we taxpayers should be pleased that the IRS has not been able to get their $4 billion computer system working properly.
—Tax expert and Stanford University professor George Marotta

Flowers

Yes, flowers are deductible, for the office, for the store, for your secretary, for a customer or client, for an office party.

Expense category: Office expense.

Food

Food samples available to the public are fully deductible. Food and beverages served at business-related events, such as a demonstration or exhibit, are deductible.

Expense category: Cost-of-goods-sold (if samples); or Advertising.

Meals are partly deductible, if they meet certain IRS requirements. See **Meals**.

Franchise Fees

Business franchise fees you pay to become a franchisee, licensee, distributor, etc., may have to be amortized (deducted) over a period of years. You should check with your accountant. Ongoing franchise fees are deductible.

Do not confuse franchise fees with franchise taxes. They are different. See **Franchise Taxes.**

Expense category: Commissions and fees.

Franchise Taxes

Franchise taxes are state taxes on corporations. Corporations are licensed by the states. Each state grants corporations what they call a franchise to do business in the state, for which they charge an annual franchise tax. Some franchise taxes are annual fees, some take the form of an income tax. They are deductible on your federal return.

Don't confuse this franchise tax with taxes on franchise businesses (McDonald's, Holiday Inn, those kinds of businesses). The word franchise has two different meanings here. All corporations, whether they are franchises or not, pay state franchise taxes.

Most states do not impose franchise taxes on unincorporated businesses. But if your unincorporated business does pay a state franchise tax, it is deductible.

Expense category: Taxes and licenses.

After spending $4 billion in a failed effort to upgrade its antiquated computers, the IRS is ready to try again, and the company that pocketed millions on the aborted Document Processing System (DPS) project, Lockheed Martin, is vying for a piece of the new multibillion-dollar job.
—Associated Press

DPS was a major software development success story for the IRS and the Treasury. *—Former Lockheed Chairman Bernard Schwartz*

Well, I don't think so.
—Former IRS Commissioner Margaret Richardson

Free Agents

Free agent is another term for independent contractor. Fees are deductible. See **Independent Contractors**.

Expense category: Commissions and fees.

Freelancers

Fees charged by freelancers and other independent professionals are deductible. See **Independent Contractors**.

Expense category: Commissions and fees.

A man murdered his wife and killed himself. Under state law where the deaths occurred, the man is treated as having died first, which denies his estate any benefit from her death. Attorney for the man's estate argued before the IRS that if the man is considered to have died first, his estate is entitled to a marital tax deduction for what she was to inherit. IRS denied the deduction. The man didn't really die first, so there is no marital deduction. —IRS Ruling 328-7448, 1998, Washington, D.C.

Freight

Freight refers to all shipping and delivery charges. Freight costs on goods you sell are fully deductible. Freight on goods you receive are deductible, with two exceptions:

Freight charges for inventory you are buying must be included as part of the cost of the inventory. See **Inventory**. Freight charges for business assets you are buying (machinery, furniture, etc.) should be added to the cost of the asset. See **Business Assets**.

Expense category: Other expenses.

Fringe Benefits

Employers can deduct the cost of employee fringe benefits, with some exceptions and limits. Fringe benefits for you, the business owner, and your family may or may not be deductible depending on how your business is structured.

See: **Awards, Business Gifts, Dependent Care, Discounts, Education, Health Insurance, Life Insurance, Medical Expenses, Medical Savings Accounts, Parking, Retirement Plans.**

See IRS Publication 15-A, "Employer's Supplemental Tax Guide."

Expense category: Employee benefit programs.

Fuel

Fuel for vehicles, aircraft and boats is deductible. See **Vehicles.** Heating fuel and other utilities are deductible.

Expense category: Utilities; Car and truck expenses.

Home-Based Businesses: You can deduct a percentage of your home utilities only if you are allowed a home office deduction. See **Home Office.** Home-office utilities are reported on Form 8829, "Expenses for Business Use of Your Home."

Manufacturers: Fuel for the manufacturing process may have to be added to the cost of the inventory rather than being written off immediately. See **Inventory.**

Furniture

Furniture can be deducted (with some limits) or depreciated. See **Business Assets.**

Expense category: Depreciation. You must also fill out Form 4562, "Depreciation and Amortization."

The law is an ass. —Mr. Bumble, in Oliver Twist.

Garbage Service

Garbage and other utilities are deductible.

Expense category: Utilities.

Home-Based Businesses: You can deduct a percentage of your home utilities only if you are allowed a home office deduction. See **Home Office**. Home-office utilities are reported on Form 8829, "Expenses for Business Use of Your Home."

Manufacturers: Garbage service for the manufacturing process may have to be added to the cost of the inventory rather than being written off immediately. See **Inventory**.

Gardening Expenses
Gardening, lawn care and landscaping expenses are deductible. Hiring a gardener (self-employed) is fully deductible.
Expense category: Repairs and maintenance.

Home-Based Businesses: Landscaping and lawn care are not deductible for home-based businesses, even if done solely to enhance the image of the business. The only exception to this rule is for home-based landscapers, if they are using the landscaping to demonstrate or advertise their services.

General Business Credit
This is not one, but several tax credits lumped under one heading. Tax credits are different than tax deductions, and can reduce your taxes significantly. See **Tax Credits**.
Expense category: Tax credits are taken on Form 1040.

Initially, Congress enacts a tax law. Then the Internal Revenue Service, either by using its regulatory authority or by making interpretive rulings, amends or repeals the legislation. Congress then adopts a new law overruling the IRS and reenacting what it said originally.
—*Society of California Accountants*

Gifts

Gifts are deductible, with certain limits. See **Business Gifts.**
Expense category: Other expenses.

Goodwill

A successful business is worth more than a new business or a failing business, because satisfied customers will continue to patronize a successful business. That intangible "worth more" is called goodwill.

There is no tax deduction for goodwill until the business is sold. A portion of the purchase price is often allocated to goodwill. It is often an arbitrary dollar figure pulled out of the air, which is probably why goodwill is also called, in business jargon, "blue sky." Goodwill "purchased" in this manner cannot be deducted immediately. It must be amortized (depreciated) over 15 years. See **Depreciation**.

Expense category: Depreciation. You must also fill out Form 4562, "Depreciation and Amortization."

Graphic Design

See **Design Costs.**

Greeting Cards

Deductible. And greatly appreciated. Send lots of greeting cards.
Expense category: Office expense.

Grooming

Personal grooming expenses are not deductible, except when travelling away from home overnight on business. See **Travel**. Grooming expenses related to a show or other promotion are deductible.
Expense category: Other expenses; or Travel (if travelling).

I'm proud to be paying taxes in the United States. The only thing is, I could be just as proud for half the money. —Early TV star Arthur Godfrey

---

Egypt's First Dynasty, 3000 B.C,. was so civilized it had deadly weapons of metal, government officials, and taxes. —Encyclopedia Britannica

Gross Receipts Tax

A gross receipts tax is a tax on total business receipts—sales, income—before any deductions for expenses. The tax is in addition to any income or sales tax. Some states call their sales tax a gross receipts tax, but the tax referred to here is not a sales tax. Sales tax is collected from your customers. Gross receipts taxes are paid out of your own pocket.

Gross receipts taxes are deductible.

Expense category: Taxes and licenses.

Group Health Insurance

Generally, the cost of group health insurance plans for your employees is deductible. Former employees and families of employees can be included. Plans where you, the employer, reimburse employees for actual out-of-pocket medical expenses, are also allowed.

Self-employed individuals cannot deduct 100% of group health insurance premiums for themselves. See **Health Insurance**.

Expense category: Employee benefit programs.

Guard Dog

The cost of buying, feeding and maintaining a watch dog is deductible. The animal itself may have to be depreciated over its expected life.

Expense category: Other expenses. Depreciation.

Gun

If having a gun is an ordinary and necessary expense of your business, it is deductible. See **Business Assets, Depreciation.**

Expense category: Depreciation. You must also fill out Form 4562, "Depreciation and Amortization."

Handicapped Access

Most structural work can be depreciated. See **Depreciation**. Cost of making a business more accessible to handicapped people may also be eligible for a special tax credit. See **Tax Credits**.

Heating

Heating and other utilities are deductible.
Expense category: Utilities.

Home-Based Businesses: You can deduct a percentage of your home utilities only if you are allowed a home office deduction. See **Home Office**. Home-office utilities are reported on Form 8829, "Expenses for Business Use of Your Home."

Manufacturers: Heating for the manufacturing process may have to be added to the cost of the inventory rather than being written off immediately. See **Inventory**.

Health Benefits

See **Health Insurance** and **Medical Expenses**.

The IRS's primary task is to collect taxes under a voluntary compliance system.

—IRS Official Annual Report to Congress

Telephone conversation between Irwin Schiff, tax crusader, and the IRS National Office, reported by Mr. Schiff's Tax Web Page:
   Mr. Schiff: Is filing an income tax return based on voluntary compliance?
   IRS: It is.
   Mr. Schiff: In that case, I don't want to volunteer.
   IRS: You have to volunteer.

Health Insurance

Self-Employed Individuals:

Sole proprietors, partners in partnerships, members of limited liability companies, and owners of S corporations can deduct 70% of the cost of health insurance for themselves, their spouses and dependents. The 70% is for 2002. Increases to 100% in 2003.

The deduction is not allowed if you are eligible for employer-paid (subsidized) health insurance through your own employer (if you have another job) or through your spouse's employer. The deduction may not exceed the net profit from your business.

Premiums for long-term care insurance can be included as part of this health insurance deduction. Long-term care insurance, however, is also subject to a dollar limitation, ranging from $220 to $2,750, depending on your age. The age and amount tables can be found in IRS Publication 535, "Business Expenses."

The deduction is taken on your 1040 return. It is not taken on your business tax return. It does not reduce your business profit.

The deduction does not apply when computing self employment tax. You pay self-employment tax based on your net profit before the health insurance deduction.

The balance of your health insurance costs (the other 30%) can also be deducted, with limitations, as a personal medical expense on Schedule A of your 1040 return if you itemize deductions.

Expense category: Not shown as a deduction on the business tax return. Deducted on the first page of the 1040 return.

The above rules do not apply to C corporations. Owners are employees. Insurance premiums are fully deductible. See below.

Employee Health Insurance:

Health and long-term-care insurance for your employees, their spouses and dependents, are 100% deductible. If you reimburse employees for medical expenses, these are also 100% deductible. The payments are not taxable to the employees.

Employers can also reimburse employees for actual medical expenses (doctor bills, hospitals, prescriptions, lab tests, etc.) for the employees and employees' families. The employer gets a full deduction, and the payments are not taxable to the employees.

As an option, an employer can reduce employees' salaries, reducing income tax for your employees and reducing payroll taxes for both you and your employees, and use the money instead to purchase health insurance for the employees, or pay employees medical expenses. The cost of the insurance and medical payments are tax deductible to the employer but not taxable to the employees.

Expense category: Employee benefit programs.

Family Employees:

If you employ your spouse or your children, officially on the payroll and doing legitimate work, they are eligible for the same 100% deductible health benefits offered to all your employees. In fact, if you employ your spouse, you also get 100% deductible coverage for yourself, instead of the 70%. Why? Your spouse is an employee, and employee's spouses are covered, and you are your spouse's spouse, so you're covered, too.

To get the 100% deduction, there must be a bona fide employer-employee relationship between you and your spouse, and your spouse cannot own part of the business. Also, all of your employees must be covered, not just your family.

The above rule is for 2002. Starting 2003, a 100% deduction applies to the entire family. Your spouse will no longer have to be on the payroll to get the full 100% deduction, and you will not be required to include your employees.

Expense category: Employee benefit programs.

C Corporations:

In a regular C corporation (not an S corporation), you, as an employee of your corporation, and your dependents are fully eligible for tax-free employee health benefits, and your corporation is allowed a full deduction for the cost. No 70% limitation. But the insurance must be available to all employees, not just yourself.

Expense category: Employee benefit programs.

Also see **Medical Expenses** and **Medical Savings Accounts**.

Thousands of small businesses contribute daily to the economic success of our nation. They pay taxes.   —Former Senator Bob Dole

---

Hobbies

No deductions are allowed for hobbies unless your hobby is earning you a little money. Any profits from your hobby are taxable just like the profits from a business. Expenses of your hobby are deductible, but only up to the amount of income. In other words, you can show a profit (and pay taxes), or break even (and pay no taxes), but you cannot declare a loss. A business that is a real business and not a hobby can show a loss and be able to use that loss to offset other income in figuring your taxes.

So when is an endeavor a hobby, and when is it a business? The IRS has a 3-year / 5-year formula: if you do not show a profit for at least three out of five consecutive years, the IRS can declare your "business" to be a hobby and disallow any losses. This is not a firm rule, however. A business can deduct losses for several years in a row without ever being challenged by the IRS. In the event of an audit, the IRS will allow the ongoing losses if they are convinced that you are operating a real business and trying, though unsuccessfully, to make a profit.

The key issue is *intent*. What are you really doing? Trying to earn some money or just having fun? It will help if your business looks like a business (licenses, ledgers, bank account, business cards, etc.) and if you're devoting time to it in a businesslike manner.

Low income taxpayers are being singled out for audits. I visited the homes of audit targets, some of whom were so poor they couldn't afford air conditioning in the sweltering Houston climate. What are we looking for with someone who does not have air conditioning?
—Houston IRS agent Jennifer Long, testifying before the Senate

---

Home Office

The term "Home Office", for this important tax law, refers to any home business space—office, workshop, studio, warehouse, retail store, showroom, etc.—and the expenses directly related to the space such as utilities, insurance, property taxes, etc. The term "home" includes a house, apartment, loft, condominium, trailer, mobile home, or boat. The term also includes any separate structure that is part of your residence such as a garage.

Failure to qualify for the home office deduction doesn't prohibit you from operating your business out of your home. It only means that one possibly large expense is not deductible on your federal income taxes. You can still deduct all legitimate business expenses other than those directly related to the business space itself.

The home-office rules apply to sole proprietors, partners, owners of S corporation, and members (owners) of LLCs. The home-office rules do *not* apply to C corporations. If you own a C corporation and work out of your home, you can either take a personal tax deduction as an employee business expense (if you are eligible and if you itemize deductions on Schedule A of your 1040 return) or you can lease the office to the corporation (at which time you as an individual have rental income to report on your personal tax return).

Regular and Exclusive Use: To be eligible for the home office deduction, a specific part of your home must be used regularly and exclusively for business. It can be a separate room or even part of a room as long as it is used for the business and nothing else. Period. No television in the office. No personal paperwork at the desk. (No games on the computer?) It can't double as a guest room, or kid's play room, or anything else, even when you are not working.

Two exceptions to the exclusive rule: One, if your home is your sole fixed location for a retail sales business and if you regularly store your inventory or your samples in your home, the expense of maintaining the storage area is deductible even if it isn't exclusive use of the space. Two, if you operate a licensed day care facility in your home, you do not have to use the space exclusively for business, but you must reduce the deduction by the percentage of time the area is not available for business use. Day care is covered more below.

Principal Place of Business: In order for your home office to be deductible, it must meet at least one of three requirements, in addition to the "regular" and "exclusive use" requirements above:

1. It must be your principal place of business, defined by the IRS as "the most important, consequential, or influential location," with the main emphasis on where you meet with customers or clients. A second, less important criteria is where you spend the most time.

2. The office must be used regularly (not just occasionally) by customers, clients, or patients, or to generate sales.

3. The office must be the sole fixed location where you conducts substantial administrative or management activities for the business: where you do your paperwork, or your research, or ordering supplies, or scheduling appointments. You don't have to do all of your administrative or management work at home. The great bulk of it must be done at home and nowhere else.

Meeting any one of the three above requirements qualifies you for a home office deduction (as long as you also meet the Regular and Exclusive Use test).

If your business is also operated out of another location such as a store, you are still eligible for a home office deduction, in addition to the cost of renting the store, if the home office meets the above requirements.

You can have a separate "principal place of business" for each trade or business you operate.

What's Deductible: Deductible home-office expenses include a percentage of your rent if you rent your home, or a percentage of the depreciation if you own your home, and an equal percentage of home utilities, property tax, mortgage interest and insurance. You can determine the percentage based on any reasonable allocation. Most people use either square footage or number of rooms in the house.

Home repairs, such as a new roof or furnace, are also partly deductible (though if they are major, they must be depreciated).

The IRS specifically prohibits deductions for landscaping and lawn care, even if done solely to enhance the business (unless you are in the landscaping business).

Business Loss: If your home business shows a loss, part of your home office expenses are not deductible this year. You may deduct all of your regular business expenses (other than expenses for the office space itself) and may deduct interest and property taxes on the office, regardless of profit or loss.

But the remaining home office expenses (including rent or depreciation, insurance, utilities, maintenance, repairs) may be deducted this year only if your business shows a profit. If the home office expenses wipe out your profit, you cannot reduce your profit below zero. In other words, you can deduct the expenses only up to the point your profit drops to zero. Any expenses you cannot deduct due to this limitation can be carried forward to the next year and deducted then, again only up to the point where they do not create a loss next year.

Homeowners: A warning. If you are eligible for the home-office deduction, you will run into serious tax complications when you sell your house. Any depreciation you were allowed must be "recaptured." This means you must add up all the depreciation you were eligible for during all the years you had a home office—*whether you took the depreciation or not!*—and pay income tax on that depreciation when you sell the house. (This law was effective May, 1997. If you were depreciating a home office before May, 1997, any depreciation prior to that date can be excluded from recapture).

Here is another tax trap. You are probably aware of the huge tax break for people who sell their homes: they don't have to pay income tax on the profit, up to as much as $500,000. But if you are deducting a home office, when you sell your home, the office portion of the home is not eligible for the tax-free exclusion. If you sell the house at a profit, you will owe taxes on the portion of the home that is your office.

You can avoid this problem. If you were not eligible for a home office deduction for at least 2 of the 5 years prior to sale, you don't have to exclude the office portion of your home from the tax-free gain. Your entire home will be considered a residence. So if you will be selling your home in the near future, be sure that at least 2 years prior to the sale you make your home office ineligible for the home office deduction (such as no longer using it exclusively for business).

These are important issues you should discuss with your accountant before you claim a home office deduction.

Child care and day care businesses: The home deduction is allowed only if your business is officially licensed. If the room or rooms (or entire house) is available and regularly used for day care throughout each business day, the IRS considers it used for the entire day. No need to prorate it for actual hours of use.

For more information, see IRS Publication 587, "Business Use of Your Home."

Expense category: Must be reported on Form 8829, "Expenses for Business Use of Your Home." Note that you do *not* report home office depreciation, utilities, property taxes, or other home office expenses on the expense categories normally used for these deductions. All home office expenses are reported on Form 8829.

The home based business is the last refuge from the bureaucratic meddling and stifling protectionism that inevitably accompany any and all government involvement. Those who long for government action on their behalf would do well to remember the axiom, For every government action, there is an overwhelming and destructive reaction.

—Home business owner Norman D. Wood

Home Owner's Fees/Associations

If your business is operated out of your home, and if you are eligible for the Home Office deduction explained above, a percentage of your home owner fees is deductible as part of the Home Office deduction. See **Home Office**.

Housing Allowances

Housing allowances provided by an employer to employees is a tax deductible expense, if the lodging meets the IRS's "ordinary" and "necessary" tests. For the lodging to be tax free to the employee, however, it must meet three additional requirements: (1) lodging is for the employer's convenience, (2) is required as a condition of employment, (3) is on the employer's business premises.

Expense category: Employee benefit programs.

HR 10 Plan

Another name for a Keogh tax-deferred retirement plan. See **Retirement Plans**.

Expense category: Deducted on the 1040 form.

IRS Service Center, Martinsburg, West Virginia

Husband on Payroll

See **Spouse**.

Illegal Expenses

Not all outlaws are criminals, but it's illegal to take a deduction for illegal expenses. Just say no deduction allowed.

Importing

Customs fees, duties and tariffs are deductible. Fees charged by customs brokers and international handlers are deductible. Instead of deducting customs fees immediately, in some cases the fees and duties can be added to the cost of inventory and written off as cost-of-goods-sold. You may want to ask your accountant about this.

Expense category: Taxes and licenses. Commissions and fees.

Improvements

Major improvements to a building that extend the life or increase the value of the property must be added to the cost of the property and depreciated along with it. A new roof, a new foundation, major remodeling, additions, a new heating system, are typical examples of major improvements. See **Depreciation**. Minor repairs and regular maintenance can be deducted.

Expense category: Repairs and maintenance; or Depreciation (you must also fill out Form 4562, "Depreciation and Amortization").

Blaming the IRS is a lot like blaming the doctor whose patient dies from an incurable disease. Tax reform, not IRS bashing, is the only way to liberate the American people from a system that is grotesquely burdensome and monstrous. —Former IRS Commissioner Fred Goldberg

---

Income Taxes

Federal income taxes are not deductible. State income taxes are deductible on your federal return. City or county income taxes, if imposed, are deductible.

Some states allow a deduction for federal income taxes on state income tax returns.

Expense category: Taxes and licenses.

Incorporation Fees

Some start-up corporate fees may have to be capitalized or deducted over a period of years. See **Start Up Costs**. Any fees, licenses, etc. after start-up are fully deductible.

Expense category: Taxes and licenses.

Independent Contractors

Independent contractors (outside contractors) are people who sell their services to other businesses on a contract basis, usually for a temporary time or for a specific project. Independent contractors are really in business for themselves, just like any other individually owned business providing a service. Most freelancers, consultants, free agents, and self-employed professionals are independent contractors.

Independent contractors are not employees. You do not withhold taxes, pay employment taxes, or file payroll tax returns. When you hire an independent contractor, you pay the contractor his or her fee in full. The fee is fully deductible.

Accountants, the IRS, and the Tax Courts have been arguing for years over who should be classified as an employee and who should be classified as an independent contractor. Entire books have been written on the independent contractor vs. employee controversy. There are serious risks to businesses that misclassify employees as independent contractors, and significant costs may be at stake. If you are unsure how to classify a worker, get advice from an accountant.

Expense category: Commissions and fees.

If the IRS had to prepare its own tax return, with the many problems we have found during our financial statement audits of the IRS, it would not pass the scrutiny of an IRS audit.
—Gregory Holloway, U.S. General Accounting Office

The IRS has been using an old system of accounting that is simply not auditable and not designed to be auditable. But now, the IRS has a new system.   *—IRS Chief Financial Officer Morgan Kinghorn*

Isn't that marvelous, taxpayers? Doesn't that just make you want to hurl your tax forms and your cardboard box full of 12,837 unintelligible tax-related pieces of paper into the air with joy? Finally, we have an Official IRS Excuse. From now on, if you have ANY problem with the IRS, and the amount in question is $63 million or less, simply state that your accounting system was "not designed to be auditable," but that you have a new tax system, and that everything will be OK next year.
—Dave Barry, Home Office Computing magazine

Individual Retirement Account

Better known as an IRA, this is a tax deferred retirement plan. See **Retirement Plans**.

Expense category: Deducted on the 1040 form.

Installment Purchases

When you buy anything in installments ("on time"), your deduction depends on what it is you are buying, and the accounting method you are using.

What are you buying? Vehicles, equipment and other business assets other than real estate can either be deducted when purchased or depreciated over a period of years. Buildings must be depreciated. See **Business Assets** and **Depreciation** for more information.

What accounting method are you using? Cash method taxpayers deduct the payments as they are made (there are some exceptions to this rule). Accrual method taxpayers deduct the entire purchase price, or begin to depreciate the full cost, when the purchase is made; as payments are made, they are not deducted a second time. Any interest or finance charges can be deducted separately.

If you don't know what the last paragraph is talking about, I'd like to take this opportunity (this second opportunity, actually) to recommend a book I wrote called *"Small Time Operator: How to Start Your Own Business, Keep Your Books, Pay Your Taxes, and Stay Out of Trouble."* It is published by Bell Springs Publishing of Willits, California (800-515-8050), and it will answer all your questions.

Most congressmen know little about the tax laws they enact.
—Society of California Accountants

Insurance

Most business-related insurance premiums are deductible. If you pay an insurance premium covering more than one year, you deduct only the current year's portion. Next year's portion can be deducted next year.

For a price, there is insurance for just about everything: fire, extended coverage, earthquake, riot, flood, earth movement, lightning, glass breakage, general liability, fire legal liability, property damage liability, products liability, malpractice, errors and omissions, professional liability, theft, business interruption, worker's compensation, medical, vehicle, environmental impairment, pollution liability, vandalism and malicious mischief, patent protection, disability, key-person life insurance, equipment breakdown, credit (accounts receivable) insurance, copyright insurance, export insurance, computer meltdown insurance, employment practices liability insurance, and (a sad sign of the times) sexual harassment insurance. There's probably even insurance that insures your insurance, in case you aren't covered when you thought you were. (No, don't write; I don't really know any company that offers such insurance.)

Expense category: Insurance.

Some types of insurance have special rules:

Vehicle insurance: Deductible only if you don't take the Standard Mileage Allowance. See **Vehicles**.

Workers' compensation insurance: Deductible for your employees. For self employed individuals, workers' compensation premiums for yourself are deductible only if your state requires you to cover yourself. If your own coverage is not required by state law, it is not deductible.

Disability insurance: Disability insurance for your employees is deductible. Disability insurance for yourself is not deductible unless you are an employee of your corporation.

Life insurance: Self employed individuals cannot deduct the cost of life insurance on themselves. Premiums for group term life insurance paid by an employer on behalf of employees are deductible, but only if the employer is not a beneficiary. If coverage exceeds $50,000, the premiums must be included in the employee's compensation as additional wages, subject to payroll taxes.

Business interruption insurance: May or may not be deductible, depending on what the insurance actually covers. You should check with your accountant on the deductibility of this kind of insurance, as the tax law gets a bit confusing.

Self Insurance: Some businesses, in lieu of buying insurance, set aside funds to cover possible losses such as fire or theft or a liability claim against the business. Some people call these funds a "reserve". The money set aside or in the reserve is not considered a business expense and is not tax deductible.

Health Insurance: Health insurance has so many rules, it has its own category. See **Health Insurance**.

Home-Based Businesses: A portion of homeowners or renters insurance is deductible if you are eligible for the home-office deduction. See **Home Office**.

Expense category: Home-office insurance is reported on Form 8829, "Expenses for Business Use of Your Home."

Intangibles

Intangibles (also called intellectual property) are business assets you cannot see, such as copyrights, trademarks, patents, goodwill. They cost money, they have value, and they can be amortized (deducted) over a period of years. Software is considered an intangible also. (Some trademark expenses can be written off when paid. See **Trademarks**).

See: **Copyrights. Goodwill. Patents. Trademarks. Software.** For more on writing off assets over a period of years, see **Depreciation**.

Expense category: Depreciation. You must also fill out Form 4562, "Depreciation and Amortization."

Accountants are boring. We hire people who have more personality.
   —John T. Hewitt, founder, Jackson Hewitt Tax Service, on hiring tax preparers without requiring them to have extensive backgrounds in tax preparation (reported in Entrepreneur magazine).

Letter to the Editor, Anderson Valley Advertiser, Boonville, CA:

Is the IRS that the mainstream press is writing about the same one I've been dealing with for 50 years? Is it the one that maintains a local office with courteous, knowledgeable people to help me with the intricacies of tax law, and that maintains an online service to provide forms and tax help?

In the mainstream articles, I don't recognize the organization that sponsors programs to help poor and low-wage and senior taxpayers. I do recognize the organization created and presented before the Senate hearings through carefully prepared, rehearsed, anonymous and unquestioned testimony, the purpose of which was to advance a less-taxes-for-corporations-and-the-wealthy Republican agenda that much of the corporate press has embraced like a mistress.

I never worked for any government agency, nor do I like paying taxes. However, the IRS doesn't create taxes, it merely collects them. In any organization there are bound to be some bad apples, but their manifestation is far more apt to be laziness than in aggressive persecution of the populace. They leave that to Congress.

—Durwald Leeper, Knoxville, Tn.

Intellectual Property

This is another term for intangibles, assets you cannot see such as goodwill, patents, trademarks and copyrights. See **Intangibles**.

Expense category: Depreciation. You must also fill out Form 4562, "Depreciation and Amortization."

Interest Expense

Interest paid on business debts, interest on credit-card purchases, and interest on purchases of business assets is deductible, with a few important exceptions.

Interest on loans to construct real estate (as opposed to buying a structure already built) must usually be capitalized; that is, added to the cost of the property and depreciated along with the property. See **Depreciation**.

Points and other loan origination fees are deductible, but the deduction must be spread out over the length of the loan.

Interest on back taxes is not deductible (except for corporations), even if the back taxes are business related.

Interest on a personal loan is deductible as a business expense if the loan was used for your business. Be sure to keep good records showing that the money was really put into your business.

On some real estate and equipment, you have the option to capitalize the interest (add it to the cost of the building or equipment) and deduct it over a period of years rather than deduct it currently. This may be advantageous to you if you are just starting out in business, are not making much money, and do not need the immediate deduction. I suggest you discuss this with your accountant.

Prepaid interest may or may not be deductible. See **Prepayments**.
Expense category: Interest.

Buying a Business: If you borrow money to purchase part or all of an existing business, the laws can get complicated. Part of the interest may be deductible as a current business expense, but part may have to be capitalized. You will probably need an accountant's help.

Corporations: How you structure corporate finances can have a major effect on how much you pay in taxes. If you are an employee of your own corporation, and you get a personal loan to purchase business assets, the interest is not deductible as a business expense. If the corporation itself borrows the money, the interest is deductible.

Why does a slight tax increase cost you $200, and a substantial tax cut save you 30 cents?

—Business owner Peg Bracken

Internet Access

The costs of Internet access are fully deductible if used only for business. If used partly for business, you must prorate the cost and deduct only the business portion.

The cost of setting up a Web page is deductible. If the amount is significant, it may have to be amortized (depreciated) over several years. You should check with your accountant on this.

Expense category: Office expense (Internet access). Advertising (Web page).

Inventory

Inventory is merchandise—goods, products, parts—held for sale in the normal course of business. Inventory also includes repair shop parts and manufacturing parts, "raw materials" and supplies that will go into the making of a finished product, and work in process (partly finished goods you are making). Display items are considered inventory if you plan to eventually sell them. Samples you give away are also considered inventory.

Not all of your inventory purchases can be deducted as current year expenses. Only the cost of those goods actually sold is deductible. This is called "cost of goods sold." There is a very important distinction between inventory and cost-of-goods-sold; you should understand it completely. The cost of inventory unsold at year-end is an asset owned by you and will not be a deductible expense until sold (or until it becomes worthless; covered below).

Cost-of-goods-sold is your most important and usually your largest item of expense. The federal income tax form has two main categories of expense: (1) cost-of-goods-sold, and (2) all other. You will be required to show on your tax return how you calculated your cost-of-goods-sold.

Calculating cost-of-goods-sold is a three-step procedure:

Step One: You start with the cost of your inventory on hand at the beginning of the year.

Step Two: You add all the inventory purchases during the year. Beginning inventory (from Step One), plus your purchases during the year, gives you the total inventory available for sale during the year.

Step Three: Subtract the ending inventory (the cost of inventory still on hand at the end of the year). The resulting figure is your cost of goods sold: Inventory at January 1 *plus* purchases during the year *minus* inventory on hand December 31 *equals* cost-of-goods-sold.

With me so far? If not, stop and go back. There aren't too many tax laws that require your full understanding, but this is one of them.

Inventory On Hand At Start of Business: If you are starting a new business and already have inventory on hand that you will be putting into the business, inventory you purchased before going into business, you can add the cost of that inventory (or the market value if less than cost) to the current year's purchases—even though you didn't buy it this year—and include it in your beginning inventory for computing the cost-of-goods-sold.

Taking Inventory: At the end of the year you will need to make a list of inventory on hand. This is called "taking inventory" or "taking a physical inventory." (Business folk use the word "inventory" to refer both to the goods and to the procedure of counting the goods.) Inventory on hand at year-end is usually valued at its cost to you and not at its sales price.

If for any reason your year-end inventory is worth less than what you paid, the inventory should be valued at this lesser amount. "Worth" refers to its retail value, what you can sell it for. If year-end inventory is totally worthless, it should be valued at zero. This inventory valuation method is known as "lower of cost or market": You value your year-end inventory at its cost or at its market value, whichever is less.

You may have figured out that reducing the value of your year-end inventory increases your cost-of-goods-sold expense, thereby decreasing your profits and your taxes.

Inventory Lost, Stolen or Given Away: The cost of stolen or missing inventory and the cost of samples given away are deductible as part of cost-of-goods-sold. This missing inventory is not on hand at year end, so it is not included in your year-end inventory count. Therefore, it automatically becomes part of your cost-of-goods-sold (even though it really wasn't sold—the term "cost-of-goods-sold" really should be "cost of goods sold, lost, stolen, given away, damaged, unsalable, etc."). No additional write-off is allowed.

Manufacturers and Crafts Businesses: Computing the cost of your inventory will be a difficult task, for two reasons. First, you must calculate the cost not only of your raw materials but of your finished and partially finished goods as well. This will require a lot of educated guesswork—it always does. Value your inventory at its cost to you.

That cost includes materials and paid labor. It does not include your own labor (unless you are an employee of your own corporation).

The other complication in computing cost-of-goods-sold is a nasty law called the Uniform Capitalization Rule. The rule applies to all manufacturers and other businesses that, to quote the IRS, "construct, build, install, manufacture, develop, improve, create, raise, or grow property." Crafts businesses come under this rule.

Under the Uniform Capitalization Rule, the cost of a manufacturer's inventory must include the cost of overhead attributable to the manufacturing operation. Such manufacturing overhead becomes part of the cost of the manufactured product, just like the cost of the materials, and cannot be deducted until the product is sold. "Overhead" in this context is very broad and refers to almost everything related to manufacturing: repairs, maintenance, utilities, rent, indirect labor and production supervisory wages, indirect materials, tools and equipment, warehousing costs, administrative costs, insurance, taxes, employee benefits, you name it.

Consignment: Consigned inventory is merchandise one business or self-employed individual places with another business for the other business to try to sell. For full information, see **Consignment**.

For more information on inventory and cost-of-goods-sold, see IRS Publication 538, "Accounting Periods and Methods."
Expense category: Cost of goods sold.

Inventory Tax

Some local and state governments impose an inventory tax (sometimes called a floor tax), a property tax on business inventory. This tax is deductible.
Expense category: Taxes and licenses.

Why, when it comes to law, I have nothing to say. For laws were never meant to be understood, and it is foolish to make the attempt.
—The Tin Woodman of Oz

Minister of War: "Enough of this. How about taking up the tax."
Groucho: "How about taking up the carpet."
Minister of War: "I insist we must take up the tax."
Groucho: "He's right. You've got to take up the tacks before you can take up the carpet."
Minister of War: "I give all my time and effort to my duties, and what do I get?"
Groucho: "You get awfully tiresome after a while."
Minister of War:" Sir, you try my patience."
Groucho: "I don't mind if I do. Come over and try mine some time."
Minister of War: "The Secretary is out of order."
Groucho: "Which reminds me, so is the plumbing."

—Duck Soup

Investment Expenses

Investment expenses, including broker fees, publications, consultants, advice, etc. are not deductible as business expenses. Investing is not considered a business activity by the IRS.

IRA

Stands for Individual Retirement Account, a tax deferred retirement plan. See **Retirement Plans**.

Expense category: Deducted on the 1040 form.

Janitorial Service

Janitorial and cleaning services are deductible.

Expense category: Office expense.

Keogh Plan

A Keogh (also known as an HR-10 plan) is a tax deferred retirement plan. See **Retirement Plans**.

Expense category: Deducted on the 1040 form.

The IRS Restructuring and Reform Act, described by the House Ways and Means Committee as, "A superb bill that protects the interests of taxpayers," and described by former President Clinton as, "Giving Americans a modern, customer-friendly IRS," also includes a little-noticed rider cutting capital gains taxes for wealthy investors, and modifying retirement rules that will, according to the Treasury Department and the IRS Commissioner, only benefit wealthy retirees.

—Associated Press

Kickbacks

Kickbacks often refer to nasty illegal payoffs, bribes, and other wonderful stuff. But sometimes the term kickback refers, rather crudely, to rebates to customers or suppliers, or commissions or rewards paid for referrals. Some states outlaw some kinds of kickbacks. Illegal expenses are not deductible. (If a payment is illegal in your state, it is not deductible on your state *or* federal return).

If the kickbacks are legal, they are deductible.

Expense category: Depends on how the money is actually spent.

Land

Land is not deductible until you sell it. Only the cost of a structure can be depreciated.

Real estate developers: Pre-development costs such as planning and design, blueprints, building permits, engineering studies, landscape plans, and the like, cannot be deducted currently, but must be capitalized.

Landscaping

Landscaping and lawn care expenses are deductible.

Expense category: Repairs and maintenance.

Home-Based Businesses: Landscaping and lawn care are not deductible for home-based businesses, even if done solely to enhance the image of the business. The only exception to this rule is for home based landscapers, if they are using the landscaping to demonstrate or advertise their services.

Real estate developers: Landscape plans cannot be deducted currently, but must be capitalized.

Late Charges

Late charges are deductible, except for government penalties. Penalties for late filing of government forms and tax returns are not deductible.

Expense category: Interest; or Other expenses.

Laundry Services

Laundry services for clothing used exclusively for work are deductible, but only if the clothing is unsuitable for street wear, such as a uniform, costume, or protective gear.

Expense category: Office expense.

Laundry services for your regular clothing are deductible if you are travelling away from home overnight on business.

Expense category: Travel.

Brilliant deduction, Dr. Watson.   —*Sherlock Holmes*

Lawn Care

Lawn care and landscaping expenses are deductible.

Expense category: Repairs and maintenance.

Home-Based Businesses: Landscaping and lawn care are not deductible for home-based businesses, even if done solely to enhance the image of the business. The only exception to this rule is for home-based landscapers, if they are using the landscaping to demonstrate or advertise their services.

Lawyers

See **Attorneys**. Or maybe don't see attorneys.

Leases

Business leases and rentals—buildings, vehicles, equipment—are deductible (but see **Automobile Leases** below). Lease-purchase arrangements are usually considered purchases, not leases, and handled like any other purchase.

Prepaid lease payments may or may not be deductible. See **Prepayments**.

Expense category: Rent or lease.

A payment made to cancel a lease is deductible. A payment made to cancel a lease in order to get a more favorable lease, must be deducted over the term of the new lease.

Expense category: Rent or lease.

Automobile leases: Automobile leases, if 30 days or longer, are not 100% deductible. The IRS has a table, called "Inclusion Amounts for Cars," that shows how much of an auto lease can and cannot be deducted. See IRS Publication 463 for the table. This rules does not apply to trucks, vans or heavy sport utility vehicles.

Leasing equipment from employees: Payments to employees for use of their equipment are considered taxable wages, not lease payments, unless the payments are part of a formal accountable plan. You should talk to an experienced accountant about this.

Just remember, the business belongs to you, not your accountant.
—Business columnist and CPA Gloria Gibbs Marullo

Legal Fees

Most legal and paralegal fees are deductible.
Expense category: Legal and professional services.

Legal fees associated with starting or buying a business cannot be deducted the year paid. They have to be capitalized or amortized over a five year period. See **Start Up Costs. Buying A Business.**

Licenses

Business licenses and permits are deductible.

Vehicle licenses are deductible if you don't take the standard mileage allowance. See **Vehicles**.

Licenses for any business property (yacht, Lear jet, junkyard dog) are deductible.

Expense category: Taxes and licenses.

Life Insurance

Self employed individuals cannot deduct the cost of life insurance on themselves. Premiums for group term life insurance paid by an employer on behalf of employees are deductible, but only if the employer is not a beneficiary. If coverage exceeds $50,000, the premiums must be included in the employee's compensation as additional wages, subject to payroll taxes.

Expense category: Insurance.

I hate the government on April 15 every year, but otherwise it leaves me alone.

—Scott Adams, creator of Dilbert

Limousine Service

Some businesses will have a special occasion to hire a limousine service, which is deductible if appropriate for your business. However, see my comments under **Chauffeur**.

Be careful if this service is considered an entertainment expense, which is only 50% deductible. See **Entertainment**.

Expense category: Legal and professional services?

Who Gets Welfare, Item #99: Archer Daniels Midland Company, who bill themselves as "The Supermarket to the World," receives $550 million a year in taxpayers' money to produce ethanol, a corn by-product.
—Reported by Women's International League for Peace and Freedom, Philadelphia, Pa.

Archer Daniels Midland, the company that advertises itself as "The Supermarket to the World" more accurately might be called "The Pickpocket to America." ADM, which manufactures 70% of America's ethanol, is a major donor to both the Democratic and Republican parties. Lasst year, ADM and the family of chairman G. Allen Andreas donated $400,000 to the two parties.
—Syndicated columnist Debra J. Saunders

The tax break [ethanol subsidy] is revenue neutral. Its removal would lower the demand for corn, thereby causing an increase in federal corn subsidies.
—U.S. Treasury Department

Loans

A loan is not income when received and not an expense when paid. Repayment of a loan (principal) is not deductible.

Interest, loan fees and closing costs may be deductible. See **Interest**. Points and other loan origination fees are deductible, but the deduction must be spread out over the length of the loan.

Expense category: Interest.

Loan Fees

Some loan fees are deductible. See **Loans. Interest.**

Expense category: Interest.

Lobbying Expenses

If you spend money to try to influence a federal or state legislator or a federal or state election, you must meet two requirements in order to deduct your expenses: (1) The total amount spent cannot exceed $2,000, and (2) The money must be spent "in house," meaning you cannot hire an outside professional lobbyist.

If part of your dues to a trade or professional association are for political lobbying, that portion of the dues is not deductible.

Lobbying and similar expenses to try to influence local legislation do not come under the above restrictions. You are allowed a deduction for lobbying (and petitioning, and meeting with, and arguing with) your county supervisors, city council members, zoning commissioners, building inspectors, fire marshals, and all those fine local folks who often have a lot of power over local businesses.

Expense category: Legal and professional services.

Political contributions are not deductible.
No deduction is allowed for bribing the judge.

Lodging

Lodging is deductible while travelling on business, but with some restrictions. Corporations can use a per diem rate in lieu of actual costs (non corporate businesses cannot use the per diem). See **Travel**.

More information: See IRS Publ. 535, "Business Expenses."
Expense category: Travel.

Lodging and housing allowances provided by an employer to employees is a tax deductible expense, if the lodging meets the IRS's "ordinary" and "necessary" tests. The lodging is also tax-free to the employee if it meets three additional requirements: (1) lodging is for the employer's convenience, (2) is required as a condition of employment, (3) is on the employer's business premises.

See IRS Publ. 15, Circular E, "Employer's Tax Guide."
Expense category: Employee benefit programs.

Every April 15, I promise myself I'll be better prepared for next year's taxes. Then I turn to some more immediate concern, like earning a living, and forget all about taxes until next April 15, when I panic again.
—Tom Person, Laughing Bear Newsletter, Houston, Tx.

Logo

The cost of creating a company or product logo is deductible. If the cost is substantial, it may have to be amortized (depreciated) over several years. You should ask your accountant about this.

Expense category: Other expenses; or, if you amortize the cost, Depreciation (you must also fill out Form 4562, "Depreciation and Amortization").

Graphic designs and package designs are deductible.

Expense category: Advertising.

Long Term Care Insurance

Sole proprietors, partners in partnerships, members of limited liability companies, and owners of S corporations can deduct up to 70% of the cost of long-term-care insurance for themselves, their spouses and dependents. The 70% is for 2002. It is scheduled to increase to 100% in 2003.

Long-term care insurance is considered part of the self-employed health insurance deduction, explained under Health Insurance.

Long-term care insurance, however, is subject to a dollar limitation, ranging from $240 to $2,990, depending on your age. The age and amount tables can be found in IRS Publication 535, "Business Expenses."

The deduction is not allowed if you are eligible for employer-paid (subsidized) long-term care insurance through your own employer (if you have another job) or through your spouse's employer. The deduction may not exceed the net profit from your business.

The deduction is taken on your 1040 return. It is not taken on your business tax return. It does not reduce your business profit.

Long-term-care insurance for your employees, their spouses and dependents, is 100% deductible, and not taxable to the employees.

Expense category: Employee benefit programs.

Special interest tax perks leave the IRS under terrific pressure to collect from ordinary Americans who don't have pals in Congress.

—Newsweek magazine

Who Gets Welfare, Item #76: Sam Donaldson, ABC News Correspondent, receives $97,000 annually of taxpayers' money from U.S. Department of Agriculture, to subsidize his sheep and angora ranch in New Mexico.
—Reported by the Women's International League for Peace and Freedom, Philadelphia, Pa.

Losses

Casualty and theft losses are deductible, with some limitations. See **Casualty Losses**.

Business losses (showing a loss on your tax return) can be used to offset other income this year, and can also be used to offset profits from other years. See **Net Operating Loss (NOL)**.

Machinery

Machinery can be deducted (with limitations) or depreciated. See **Business Assets** and **Depreciation**.

Expense category: Depreciation. You must also fill out Form 4562, "Depreciation and Amortization."

Magazines

Books, magazines, newsletters, newspapers, and all other publications are deductible.

Expense category: Office expense.

Mailing Lists

Mailing list rentals and purchases are deductible.

Expense category: Advertising

Mailing Supplies and Expenses

Fully deductible.

Expense category: Advertising.

A former IRS official has admitted cashing taxpayers' checks by changing IRS on the checks to his name, J.R. Stevens. Stevens pleaded guilty Friday to embezzling $77,218 by cashing 13 checks. The 13 cases involved treasurer's and cashier's checks, which are not routinely sent back to the check writer. The scheme was uncovered a year ago by a Baltimore lawyer when Stevens failed to correct the lawyer's tax records after cashing a $6,578 check. The IRS was not aware of the embezzlement until the lawyer filed a complaint. —Associated Press, Baltimore

Maintenance

Maintenance and minor repairs are deductible.
Expense category: Repairs and maintenance.

Major repairs that add to the value or extend the useful life of an asset must be treated as a permanent investment and handled in the same manner as the purchase of a depreciable asset. See **Business Assets** and **Depreciation**.
Expense category: Depreciation. You must also fill out Form 4562, "Depreciation and Amortization."

Manufacturers: Maintenance of manufacturing facilities may have to be added to the cost of your inventory rather than being deducted immediately. See **Inventory**.

Manufacturing Supplies

Manufacturing supplies are deductible, but manufacturing supplies that go into the product being manufactured are part of your inventory and cannot be deducted until sold. See **Inventory**.
Expense category: Supplies; or Cost of goods sold.

Market Research

Market research expenditures may be deductible currently, or they may have to be capitalized and deducted over a period of years, depending on their nature and the cost.

Market research for a business you haven't yet started may or may not be deductible. See **Start-Up Costs**.

Market research is not eligible for the Research Tax Credit.

Expense category: Varies depending on actual expenses.

Marketing

Marketing is a broad term that includes advertising, promotion, entertainment, news releases, catalogs, you name it. Except for entertainment (which is 50% deductible), most marketing expenses are fully deductible, but not as a lump sum. Look up each item that comprises your marketing expenses to see what is and is not deductible.

I hold in my hand 1,379 pages of tax simplification.
—*Former Congressman Del Latta*

Materials and Supplies

Some materials and supplies are deductible, but some must be included in inventory. See **Manufacturing Supplies. Office Supplies. Shipping Supplies.**

Meals

Regular meals at work are generally not deductible.

Meals with a current or prospective customer are 50% deductible, but only if business is specifically discussed at the meal and if the cost is not "lavish or extravagant." You must have a receipt and write on it who you took out and why. Tips are considered part of the meal and are also 50% deductible. (Travel to and from the restaurant, including parking, is 100% deductible).

Expense category: Meals and entertainment.

Meals while traveling away from home on business are 50% deductible.

Expense category: Meals and entertainment.

Meals that are included as part of a business meeting or seminar and not billed separately, are probably fully deductible. The IRS has not clearly ruled on this issue, so check with your accountant.

Expense category: Other expenses.

Meals provided by an employer to employees are not deductible unless the meals are on the business premises, and are for "the convenience of the employer." There must be a substantial business reason for providing the meals, such as requiring the employees to be on call. If these requirements are met, the cost of employee meals is 100% deductible.

Employers can deduct the cost of a company cafeteria if more than 50% of the meals eaten there were for the employer's convenience.

Occasional meals provided to employees, such as a pizza party, the annual company picnic, or Thanksgiving turkeys you give your employees, *are* fully (100%) deductible.

For more information, see IRS Publication 535, "Business Expenses."

Expense category: Employee benefit programs.

Hotels and Resorts: If you provide meals to employees on your business premises and on company time, you may be entitled to a partial or full deduction for the cost of the meals. Ask your accountant about this.

Interstate truck drivers whose work hours are regulated by the U.S. Department of Transportation: You can deduct 65% of the cost of meals (instead of 50%) while on the road.

Expense category: Meals and entertainment.

Food samples available to the public are fully deductible. Food and beverages served at business-related events, such as a demonstration or exhibit, are deductible.

Expense category: Cost-of-goods-sold (if samples); or Advertising.

In the long run, government is the exact symbol of its people, with their wisdom and unwisdom. We have to say, Like People, Like Government.
—Thomas Carlyle, 1844

Medical Expenses

For the purpose of this deduction, the term "medical expenses" refers to actual medical costs paid to doctors, hospitals, pharmacies, etc. but not medical insurance. Medical insurance comes under a different set of rules. See **Health Insurance**.

Employers are allowed a full deduction for employees' medical expenses, and for medical expenses of their spouses and dependents.

All businesses other than regular C corporations: You cannot take a deduction for your own medical expenses (again, we are not talking about medical insurance) unless you are an employee of your own regular C corporation. If, however, your spouse is on your payroll, your own medical expenses can also be deducted, utilizing the same loophole discussed under "Family Employees" in **Heath Insurance.**

C Corporations: If you are an employee of your own C corporation (not S corporation), your and your family's medical expenses can be deducted, but only if you offer the same medical coverage to your employees.

Expense category: Employee benefit programs.

Marry your car. Assuming your car produces no income and the two of you file jointly, you can save up to 50% of your tax bill.
—Jon Kelly, Third Runner Up in Dave Barry's Amateur Tax Tips Contest (from Home Office Computing magazine)

Medical Insurance
Fully or partly deductible. See **Health Insurance.**

Medical Savings Accounts (MSA)
A Medical Savings Account (MSA) is a special IRS-authorized account, similar to an IRA retirement account, used to pay medical bills. Businesses can set up Medical Savings Accounts to help pay medical expenses (but not health insurance) for business owners and employees. Contributions to an MSA are deductible for the employer but not taxable to the employees. Withdrawals for medical expenses are also tax-free. Medical Savings Accounts may be a less expensive alternative to employee health insurance. Most MSAs are offered by insurance companies and banks, who can give you full details.

Unless Congress passes an extension, new MSAs will no longer be offered after December 31, 2002.

More information, see IRS Publ. 969, "Medical Savings Accounts."

Expense category: Deducted on the 1040 form. You also must fill out Form 8853, "Medical Savings Accounts."

Medicare Tax

Medicare and Social Security are the two combined payroll taxes deducted from every employee's paycheck and collected from every employer. This tax is also called FICA (which stands for Federal Insurance Contributions Act) or just Social Security. Employer's portion is deductible. See **Social Security Tax**.

Expense category: Taxes and licenses.

The power to tax involves the power to destroy.
—*Chief Justice John Marshall, 1819*

Meetings

Business meetings are deductible, although you are allowed only a 50% deduction for meals. See: **Travel. Meals. Lodging.**

Expense category: Other expenses.

Membership Fees

Membership fees for business groups, professional organizations, merchant and trade associations, chambers of commerce, etc. are deductible. Membership fees to community service organizations, such as Rotary, Lions, etc., are also deductible.

Membership fees in clubs run for pleasure, recreation, or other social purposes are not deductible. These include athletic, luncheon, hotel, airline, sporting and other entertainment or recreational organizations, associations, clubs and facilities. Even if you use a club membership solely to generate or discuss business, the membership fees are not deductible.

Expense category: Other expenses.

Merchandise

Merchandise is another word for inventory, goods for sale. It cannot be deducted until sold. See **Inventory**.

Expense category: Cost of goods sold.

Merchant Associations
Dues and meetings are deductible.
Expense category: Other expenses.

If part of your merchant association dues are for political lobbying, that portion of the dues is not deductible.

Messenger Service
Messenger services are deductible. (This item is dedicated to the memory of John Cipollina).
Expense category: Office expense.

The current tax system is defended by no one. I don't believe it can be fixed. We must tear the income tax out by its roots so that it can never grow back again. —Former Congressman Bill Archer

When Bill Archer, who now advocates tearing up the tax code, was Chairman of the House Ways and Means Committee he led the fight to pass the most complex tax law in U.S. history, the infamous 1,248 page Taxpayer "Relief" Act. —Reported in Newsweek Magazine

---

Mileage Allowance
The IRS has a standard mileage allowance deduction for every business mile driven. This allowance is in lieu of actual vehicle expenses such as gas, oil changes, maintenance, and the cost of the vehicle. See **Vehicles** and **Standard Mileage Allowance**.
Expense category: Car and truck expenses.

Miscellaneous
Although there must be a hundred or more miscellaneous expenses a business can legitimately deduct, it is not a good idea to label anything "miscellaneous" on your tax return. The word mis-

cellaneous is vague and can easily invite all kinds of questions from a suspicious auditor, especially if the dollar amounts are significant. It is better to use several smaller, more specific categories, and individually list them on your tax return under "Other Expenses."

Pay your taxes. Al Capone didn't get busted for all the murders he was responsible for. Like Heidi Fleiss, he was convicted for tax evasion.
—Advice to prostitutes, from Catherine La Croix,
author of "Working Girl"

Mobile Home

There are two categories of tangible assets: real property, and personal property. Real property refers to real estate, such as buildings and land. Personal property refers to all tangible property other than real estate. Real property comes under different tax rules than personal property.

A mobile home can be either real property or personal property, depending on several factors. If the mobile home is permanent, mounted on a foundation, hooked up to utilities, it is usually considered real property. If the mobile home is in a temporary location, still on wheels, easily movable, it is usually considered personal property.

An important consideration is how the mobile home is licensed and taxed by your state and county. If the mobile home is registered with the Department of Motor Vehicles, licensed as a movable trailer, it is usually considered personal property. If the mobile home is on the county property tax rolls as a structure, it is usually considered real property.

All real property must be depreciated. Personal property can be depreciated, or at your option, part or all of the cost can be deducted the year of purchase. So, a permanent mobile home must be depreciated. A movable, licensed mobile home can either be depreciated or deducted the year of purchase (up to a maximum amount).

Since personal property can give you a much bigger deduction this year than real property, it may at first appear beneficial to have your mobile home licensed by the Department of Motor Vehicles and declared to be personal property. But most personal property is subject to sales tax, and most buildings are exempt from sales tax. If the mobile will be sold and resold, you will save a fortune in sales tax if the mobile is considered real property.

Expense category: Depreciation. You must also fill out form 4562, "Depreciation and Amortization."

We've certainly sunk to idiotic levels here.
 —Michael Collins, co-chair of the Maryland ethics committee, on a tax law covering a lobbyist's wedding gift to his daughter because she is also a lobbyist and is marring a lawmaker.

Mortgages

The mortgage on business property has to be split into its components: buildings, land, taxes, insurance, interest. Each component comes under different rules. Look each item up.

Motorcycles

Motorcycles used for business can be deducted or depreciated like other vehicles. Vehicles have special limitations. See **Vehicles**.

Expense category: The category "Car and truck expenses" is for all vehicle expenses except the cost of the vehicle itself, which is deducted or depreciated under "Depreciation." (you must also fill out Form 4562, "Depreciation and Amortization").

Moving Expenses

You may deduct all the expenses of moving your business from one location to another.

Home-based businesses: The business portion of the move is fully deductible, if you are allowed the home office deduction. See **Home Office.**

Expense category: Other expenses.

Once you become knowledgeable about the law, you can make the government agents go after the real criminals and leave law abiding people like yourself alone. —Peyman Mottahedeh, dean, registrar and sole professor at Freedom Law School, Tustin, Ca.

Music System

The office music system can be deducted or depreciated, as long as it is not, to quote the IRS, "lavish or extravagant under the circumstances." See **Business Assets** and **Depreciation**.

Expense category: Depreciation. You must also fill out Form 4562, "Depreciation and Amortization."

The cost of CDs, tapes and albums is deductible.
Expense category: Office expense.

Net Operating Loss (NOL)

If your business suffers a loss this year, you will owe no income taxes on the business, which I'm sure you know. You may not know that this loss will also offset other income, such as a salary from an outside job or your spouse's wages, and reduce this year's income tax.

You can also use this year's loss to offset income, and reduce taxes, from other years. You are allowed to carry back what the IRS calls a Net Operating Loss (NOL) to apply against prior income and receive a refund of prior years' taxes, even if you were not in business then. The loss can be carried back two years. And if your taxable income for the two prior years is not sufficient to absorb the entire loss, you may carry the balance forward to apply to as many as 20 future years. At your option, you can forego the two-year carry-back period and apply your NOL entirely to the 20 future years.

An NOL, like any other tax deduction, is worth more in a high income year. If the two preceding years generated little or no income tax, you probably will do better to forego the carry-back, and apply the entire NOL to future years. Also, that way you avoid filing an amended return, which starts the IRS audit statute of limitations running again.

Net Operating Loss is not simply the business loss shown on your tax return. It is a complicated combination of business and non-business income and deductions. I don't include the NOL calculations because they are quite complex, and there's no way to simplify the procedure. Step-by-step instructions are explained in IRS Publication #536, "Net Operating Losses." Don't be put off by their complexity; the NOL deduction may save you a bundle in income taxes.

Expense category: For carrybacks, use Form 1045, "Application for Tentative Refund." For carryforward, individuals use "Other income" line on Form 1040; corporations use "Net operating loss deduction" line on Form 1120.

Law is not a profession at all, but rather a repair shop.

—Adlai Stevenson

Newsletters

Books, magazines, newsletters, newspapers, and all other publications are deductible.

Expense category: Office expense.

Newspapers

Books, magazines, newsletters, newspapers, and all other publications are deductible.

Expense category: Office expense.

NOL

NOL stands for Net Operating Loss. See **Net Operating Loss**.

Notes

Promissory notes and notes payable are not deductible, but the interest is.

Expense category: Interest.

"You're saying that as a professional writer, your expenses totaled $22,000 more than your INCOME? What kind of way is that to make a living?"

OASDI

OASDI stands for Old Age, Survivors, and Disability Insurance. OASDI is another name for the combined Medicare and Social Security payroll taxes deducted from every employee's paycheck and collected from every employer. Employer's portion of OASDI is deductible. See **Social Security Tax.**

Expense category: Taxes and licenses.

Occupational

Occupational licenses, fees, registrations, etc. are deductible.

Expense category: Taxes and licenses.

Some tax cutting strategies are simply bad ideas because tax considerations are allowed to override basic economics.

—CPA James Angell, Willits, California

"Off The Books" Payments

"Books" is another term for ledgers. "Off the books" refers to a payment, in cash, that you intentionally chose not to record in your ledgers. And now you want to find out if it is deductible? Was the payment legal? If it was legal, it probably is deductible. If it was illegal it is not deductible. For more great information about off-the-books payments, see **Under The Table,** which means the same thing.

Expense category: Varies depending on actual expenses.

Office

The cost of renting an office is deductible. The cost of an office building you own can be depreciated. See **Buildings**. The cost of a home office is deductible only if you meet the home office requirements. See **Home Office**.

Expense category: Rent or lease (for rented space); Depreciation (owned building); Form 8829, "Expenses for Business Use of Your Home" (for home based businesses).

In the 1950s, the corporate income tax was 25% of the federal outlay. It's now about 6% or 7%. This is in a period of record corporate profits, record stock market prices, record executive compensation. It is hard to find a major fortune in America that hasn't benefitted by special-interest tax legislation. So when people ask, "Why should the rich pay a larger percent of their income than middle-income people," my answer is not an answer most people get: It's because their wealth developed from laws that enriched them.

—Ralph Nader

Office Equipment

Office equipment can, at your option, be deducted the year of purchase (up to a dollar maximum) or depreciated. See **Business Assets** and **Depreciation**.

Expense category: Office expense (minor purchases); or Depreciation (also fill out Form 4562, "Depreciation and Amortization").

Office equipment includes:

Adding machines
Answering machines
Brooms
Cabinets
Calculators
Carts
Cash registers
Chair mats
Chairs
Clocks
Coat racks
Coffee makers
Computers
Copiers
Credit card terminals
Credit card imprinters
Desks
Fans
Fax machines
File cabinets
Humidifiers
Lamps
Microwave
Mirrors
Modems
Music Systems
Phones
Portable heaters
Postage meters
Printers
Racks
Refrigerators
Rugs
Scales
Shelves
Tables
Typewriters
Vacuum cleaners
Wall & office decorations
   (But see **Art Treasures**)
Waste baskets
Water dispensers
Window shades & blinds
And the office pinball machine

Office in the Home

Deductible, if it meets certain requirements. See **Home Office**.

Tax laws are complicated and unfriendly. Figuring out whether a home office can be deducted is a more difficult question than balancing the national budget. So most of us just give up and pay the full tax.
     —*Tom Person, Laughing Bear Newsletter, Houston, Tx.*

Office Supplies

"Office supplies" is a catch-all term. I tend to lump all kinds of low-cost business purchases in this category. It is a reasonably accurate description, and sure sounds better and less dubious than "Miscellaneous." Office supplies are deductible.

Expense category: Office supplies.

Office supplies include:

Account books
Bank checks
Batteries
Beverages
Blades
Books
Bottled water
Boxes
Brooms
Business cards
Carpal tunnel
  wrist supports
Cartons
Calendars
CDs
Cleaning supplies
Clipboards
Coffee
Computer disks
Directories
Dust covers
Dust pans
Envelopes
Erasers
Fasteners
File holders
Fire extinguisher
First aid kit
Flashlight
Folders
Forms

Glue
Goldfish bowls
Greeting cards
Hole punchers
Invoices
Kleenex
Knives
Labels
Ledger paper
Ledgers
Letter openers
Light bulbs
Magazines
Maps
Moisteners
Mops
Newsletters
Organizers
Paper
Paper clips
Pencils
Pens
Periodicals
Plants
Plant hangers
Post-Its
Postage stamps
Printer ribbons
Rolodex
Rubber bands
Rubber stamps

Rulers
Safety glasses
Scissors
Signs
Soap
Software
  (inexpensive)
Small tools
Stamp pads
Staple removers
Staplers
Staples
Stationery
Tape
Tape dispensers
Toner
Towels
Typewriter ribbon
Videos
Wall and office
  decorations
White-out
And most important, Emergency Rations:
Emergency box of
  chocolates
Emergency bag of
  peanuts
Emergency bottle
  of brandy

Operating Losses

Business losses (showing a loss on your tax return) can be used to offset other income this year, and can also be used to offset profits from other years. See **Net Operating Loss**.

Expense category: For carrybacks, use Form 1045, "Application for Tentative Refund." For carryforward, individuals use "Other income" line on Form 1040, corporations use "Net operating loss deduction" line on Form 1120.

Every year, the IRS sends out 8 billion pages of forms and instructions. 293,760 trees must be cut down every year to supply the paper.
—Robert Hall and Alvin Rabushka, Hoover Institute, Stanford

Organizational Costs

Most organizational costs must be amortized (depreciated) over a period of years. See **Start Up Costs**.

Expense category: Depreciation. You must also fill out Form 4562, "Depreciation and Amortization."

Organizations

Dues and other expenses for business groups, professional organizations, merchant and trade associations, chambers of commerce, etc. are deductible. Dues to community service organizations, such as Rotary, Lions, etc., are also deductible. Dues and membership fees in organizations run for pleasure, recreation, or other social purposes are not deductible. These include athletic, luncheon, hotel, airline, sporting and other entertainment or recreational organizations, associations, clubs and facilities. Even if you use your membership solely to generate or discuss business, the dues are not deductible. Sometimes the term "business club" is used to describe such a facility. If the "business" club is not a business organization, the dues are not deductible.

The cost of attending meetings and seminars are also deductible, although you are allowed only a 50% deduction for meals.

See: **Travel. Meals. Lodging.**

Expense category: Other expenses.

If part of your dues to a trade or professional association or other organization are for political lobbying, that portion of the dues is not deductible.

Other Expenses

I list this because there is a category on the tax return called Other Expenses. But you should not label any expenses "Other Expenses." Like the category Miscellaneous, "other" is too vague, and can easily invite questions from a suspicious IRS auditor, especially if the dollar amounts are significant. It is okay to list expenses under "Other Expenses" on your tax return, but spell out what the expenses are actually for.

Expense category: Other expenses.

You will never get audited if you write possibly insane statements all over the margins of your tax return, like, "The CIA is monitoring my shoes and you know it!"

—John Averill, Second Runner Up, Dave Barry's Amateur Tax Tips Contest, Home Office Computing magazine

---

Outside Contractors

"Outside" refers not to the great outdoors, but to outside the business, not an employee. The terms outside contractor and independent contractor are used interchangeably. The term "free agent" means the same thing. Fees paid to outside contractors are deductible. See **Independent Contractors**.

Expense category: Commissions and fees.

Outstanding Checks

Outstanding checks are checks you have written that have not been deposited or cashed yet. Sooner or later, the checks almost always get deposited or cashed. Give them a little more time to see if they'll come back with your next your bank statement. If they don't, see **Uncashed Checks**.

Overhead

Overhead is a broad term and usually refers to your fixed costs, the dozens of large and small expenses you must pay whether you are generating income or not: rent, utilities, phone, insurance, office supplies, permits and licenses, payroll, and the cost and maintenance of furniture, tools and equipment. These costs cannot be tied directly to a product or service.

Most overhead is deductible, but not as a lump sum. Look up each item that comprises your overhead to see what is and isn't deductible.

Manufacturers: Manufacturing overhead is not deductible immediately. It is added to the cost of your inventory. See **Inventory**.

Of course lower taxes were promised, but that has been promised by every president since Washington crossed the Delaware in a rowboat. But taxes have gotten bigger and their boats have gotten larger until now the president crosses the Delaware in his private yacht. —Will Rogers, 1928

Read my lips: No new taxes.
—President George Bush, Sr., 1990, just before signing a tax increase

Not over my dead body will they raise your taxes.
—President George W. Bush, 2002

Owner's Draw

The owner of an unincorporated business (sole proprietorship, partnership, or limited liability company) cannot get a tax-deductible salary or wage. Payments to owners are known as "draw." See **Draw** and **Paying Yourself**.

Package Design Costs

See **Design Costs**.

Packaging Materials

Cartons, boxes, bottles, and other containers and packaging materials that are used to hold the goods you sell, are considered inventory. See **Inventory**. If, however, the cost of the containers or packaging are not significant or used only occasionally, most businesses write them off currently as shipping supplies.

Expense category: Supplies.

Painting

A minor or inexpensive paint job can be deducted currently. A major paint job that extends the life of a building or adds to the value of a building may have to be written off over a period of years. See **Depreciation**.

Expense category: Repairs and maintenance; or Depreciation (you must also fill out Form 4562, "Depreciation and Amortization").

Paralegal Fees

Paralegal fees are deductible. But see **Start Up Costs**.

Expense category: Legal and professional fees.

Parents on Payroll

Children who hire their parents get no special tax breaks. The parents are considered regular employees, subject to all regular employment and income taxes, except Federal Unemployment Tax (FUTA). Parents are exempt from FUTA tax.

Expense category: Wages.

Who Gets Welfare, Item #58: Gallo Winery of Northern California received $4.2 million in taxpayers' money over a two-year period to advertise its brandy and wine overseas. —Reported by the Boston Globe

Parking

Parking is deductible. Sometimes the simple things in life are the nicest. If you take the standard mileage allowance, parking is deductible in addition to the mileage allowance. Parking tickets are not deductible (towing charges are).

Expense category: Car and truck expenses.

Employers: If you provide parking to employees on or near your business, the costs are deductible. If the costs do not exceed $185 per month per employee, the parking is tax-free to the employee.

Expense category: Employee benefit programs.

Parking Lots

You can deduct the costs of maintaining a parking lot or parking area on your business property. Cost of constructing a parking lot or area must be depreciated. See **Depreciation**.

Expense category: Repairs and maintenance; or Depreciation (you must also fill out Form 4562, "Depreciation and Amortization").

Parking Tickets

Not deductible. Fines for breaking the law are not deductible.

Parties

A company or holiday party where all employees are invited is 100% deductible.

A sales meeting, show, or exhibit that includes refreshments, if it is primarily a business event where business is conducted, is 100% deductible.

Business parties, luncheons, dinners, or events that are primarily parties, even though thrown to promote your business, come under entertainment and are 50% deductible. See **Entertainment.**

Expense category: Office expense; Advertising; or Entertainment.

In 2000, Enron reported sales of $100 billion and profits of $979 million. Enron paid no Federal taxes. It received $382 million in tax refunds. The company used 881 subsidiaries in tax haven countries to hide income.
—From an article in the San Francisco Chronicle (that appeared on the same page of the paper with another article headlined, "IRS Plans 50,000 Random Audits of Individual Tax Returns.")

Enron and its executives contributed $5.8 million to political war chests, including donations to 71 senators and 188 house members. Enron was the top donor to George W. Bush throughout his political career. Enron's largesse with elected officials has left a widespread impression that it paid the cops on the beat to take a nap. No corporation was more political in gaming the system to get the rules written in its favor.   —Business Week

If everybody did what is alleged in the Enron episode, our system could not work. I tried to find an economic reason why those subsidiaries were created and I could not. The reason was the obvious one.
—Federal Reserve Chairman Alan Greenspan

Enron is a story about big dollars that influence public decisions.
—Representative Christopher Shays (R-Conn.)

Enron didn't get any special deals.   —Vice President Dick Cheney

Enron's failure is a tribute to American capitalism.
—White House Economic Advisor Lawrence B. Lindsey (who was paid $50,000 for work on an Enron advisory board, at the same time he was keeping watch on Enron as the Economic Advisor to President Bush.)

There is no hint of any wrongdoing.
—White House Spokesman Art Fleischer

Parts

Parts that a repair shop sells or uses, and parts that a go into a manufactured product are inventory, and cannot be deducted until sold. See **Inventory**.

Expense category: Cost of goods sold.

Parts that go into machinery or equipment that your business owns and uses (not for sale) can be deducted. If the parts are expensive and used for a major repair job, however, the parts may have to be depreciated. See **Repairs. Business Assets. Depreciation.**

Expense category: Repairs and maintenance; or Depreciation. (you must also fill out Form 4562, "Depreciation and Amortization").

Patents

Patent fees must be amortized (depreciated) over their useful life, which can be as long as twenty years.

Some of the costs of researching and designing whatever is being patented may have to be deducted over several years, and some of the costs can be deducted currently. Check with your accountant.

Expense category: Depreciation. You must also fill out Form 4562, "Depreciation and Amortization."

Paying Yourself

If your business is a sole proprietorship, partnership, or limited liability company, you the owner (or co-owner) are not an employee of your business. You cannot hire yourself as an employee. This is a point of law often misunderstood by new business people. You cannot pay yourself a wage and deduct it as a business expense.

You may withdraw (that is, pay yourself) as much or as little money as you want, but this "draw" is not a wage, you do not pay payroll taxes on it, and you cannot claim a business deduction for it. The profit of your business, which is computed without regard to your draws, is your "wage" and is included on your personal income tax return.

Corporations: If your business is a corporation, you are an employee of your business. Your salary is a deductible expense of your business.

Expense category: Wages.

Fifteen million tax returns, Sacramento, California

Payroll

Employee wages are deductible. Payroll taxes that you, the employer, pay on behalf of your employees, such as Social Security, Medicare and other federal or state requirements, are also deductible.

If your business is a sole proprietorship, partnership or limited liability company, you the owner are not an employee of your business. You cannot hire yourself as an employee. You cannot pay yourself a wage and deduct it as a business expense. You may withdraw (that is, pay yourself) as much or as little money as you want, but this "draw" is not a wage, you do not pay payroll taxes on it, and you cannot claim a business deduction for it. The profit of your business, which is computed without regard to your draws, is your "wage" and is included on your personal income tax return.

If your business is a corporation, you are an employee of your business and your salary (and payroll taxes) are a deductible expense of your business.

For more information, see IRS Publication 15, "Circular E, Employer's Tax Guide."

Expense category: Wages.

Look, we play "The Star Spangled Banner" before every game. You want us to pay income taxes, too?

—Bill Veeck, legendary owner, Cleveland Indians

Payroll Services

Payroll services are deductible.

Expense category: Legal and professional services.

Payroll Taxes

Payroll taxes that you the employer pay on behalf of your employees, such as Social Security, Medicare, and other federal or state requirements, are fully deductible.

Payroll taxes that you pay on your own wages are deductible only if your business is a corporation. If your business is a sole proprietorship, partnership or limited liability company, you the owner (or co-owner) cannot deduct your own payroll (self-employment) taxes. However, you are allowed a tax deduction on your personal 1040 return for part of the self-employment tax you pay. See **Self Employment Tax.**

Expense category: Taxes and licenses.

Payroll taxes you withhold from employees' wages are not deductible. You are entitled to a deduction for the full wages you pay, before deducting the taxes.

For example, let's say you have one employee who earns $2,000 a month. Out of that $2,000, you deduct $150 federal income tax withholding and $153 for Social Security, giving your employee take home pay of $1,697. You write your employee a paycheck for $1,697 ($2,000 - $150 - $153 = $1,697). You (the employer) get a payroll tax deduction for $2,000, not $1,697.

When you send the withheld $303 ($150 plus $153) to the IRS, you do not get a second deduction. You *do* get an additional deduction for the employer's portion of the employment taxes, the $153 Social Security you must pay out of your own pocket. (Social Security/Medicare tax on employee wages is 7.65% paid by the employee, and another 7.65% paid by the employer. 7.65% of $2,000 is $153.)

Penalties

Tax penalties and fines for violation of the law are not deductible. Penalties for not meeting contract requirements, and any other fines or penalties that do not involve breaking the law, are deductible.

Expense category: Other expenses.

Pension Plans

Many employee pension plans are deductible, but you should discuss your plans with an accountant before making any decisions. Also see **Retirement Plans**.

Expense category: Employee benefit programs; or Pensions and profit sharing plans.

It could probably be shown by facts and figures that there is no distinctly native American criminal class except Congress.

—Mark Twain

Per Diem

"Per diem" is French, or maybe Latin, for "by the day," a daily allowance. The IRS has established per-diem lodging and food deductions for people travelling away from home overnight on business.

Food and lodging per diems apply to corporations and to employees only. Self-employed individuals can use the food, but not the lodging per diems. See **Standard Meal Allowance**. For rates and details, see IRS Publ. 1542, "Per Diem Rates." Also see **Travel**.
Expense category: Travel.

Periodicals

Business periodicals, magazines, newsletters, newspapers, etc. are deductible.
Expense category: Office expense.

Permits

All business permits and licenses are deductible.
Expense category: Taxes and licenses.

Who Gets Welfare, Item #44: In one recent year, McDonald's Corporation received $466,000 in taxpayers' money to pay for advertising Chicken McNuggets in Turkey. Last year they received another $2 million to advertise in third world countries.

—Reported by the Boston Globe

Personal Property

In tax law, personal property refers to tangible business assets other than real estate. Business machinery, equipment, tools, furniture, etc. are personal property. In this context, the word "personal" does not refer to non-business.

Personal property can be deducted the year acquired or depreciated over several years, depending on several factors. See **Business Assets** and **Depreciation**.

Expense category: Depreciation. You must also fill out Form 4562, "Depreciation and Amortization."

We have reached a point where further patchwork will only compound the problem. It's time to repeal the Internal Revenue Code and start over.
—Former IRS Commissioner Shirley Peterson

Personal Property Tax

Some states and localities have a property tax on business assets such as machinery and furniture, similar to the property tax on real estate. This is known as a personal property tax (see **Personal Property** above). Although the tax uses the word "personal," this is a not a tax on non-business property. This is a business tax, and it is fully deductible.

By the way, personal property taxes can be quite high if your assets are assessed at a high value. You should examine the personal property tax bill, and make sure retired or sold assets are not included, and that older assets are not overvalued.

Expense category: Taxes and licenses.

Petty Cash

Petty cash is a small fund of cash some businesses keep on hand to pay small expenses. The expenses are usually for office supplies and are deductible. See **Office Supplies.**

Expense category: Office expense.

Plants

Office plants and their upkeep (the growing kind, not boilers and electricity-generating plants) are fully deductible.

Expense category: Office expense.

Nurseries: Plants are considered inventory. See **Inventory**. Some plant production costs, however, are currently deductible. You should consult an accountant familiar with the nursery business, as there are special IRS rules for nursery businesses.

Points

Points and other loan origination fees are deductible, but the deduction must be spread out over the length of the loan.

Expense category: Interest.

I'm not his father, and he doesn't need a nursemaid. I just tell him, Don't forget to pay your taxes. I tell him that every week when he's working. I've seen too many people get into bad trouble by forgetting to pay their taxes.
—Elvis Presley's long time manager, Col. Tom Parker, 1960

Political Contributions

Political campaign contributions, to a candidate or to a political party, are not deductible. Advertising in a political program or buying tickets to a political event are also not deductible. So how do all these huge corporations funnel hundreds of thousands of dollars into political campaigns to try to buy elections?

Lobbying expenses are sometimes deductible. See **Lobbying Expenses**.

Pollution Cleanup

See **Contamination Cleanup**.

Post Office Box

Post office box rents and mail-box store rents ("suites" as the mail order connoisseurs call them), are deductible.

Expense category: Office expense.

Postage

Postage, post office box rents, and postal permits are deductible.

Expense category: Office expense.

After the Congressional hearings, the IRS is trying to change its image. At the San Francisco Internal Revenue Service office, now renamed the IRS Customer Service Center, lobby signs now read "Please Wait Here" instead of "Wait Here." Agents wear colorful buttons that say, "We Work for You." The IRS has made other changes. It no longer audits taxpayers, it "conducts examinations." The examinations are conducted by IRS auditors and they are just the same as what used to be called audits, its just that they aren't called audits anymore. As for quotas, they don't exist either. "We don't have quotas," IRS spokesman Larry Wright said, "The term we use is compliance statistics." Have A Nice Day.   —San Francisco Chronicle

Prepayments

Prepaid expenses that cover more than twelve months cannot be deducted until the year the expenses apply to. Only the current year's portion can be written off this year. This law applies even if your business keeps books on the cash basis.

For practical purposes, minor prepayments such as for office supplies, a service contract, Internet access, etc. are written off by most businesses when paid.

Tax law specifically states that prepaid interest, prepaid rent on business property, prepaid insurance, and prepaid property taxes cannot be deducted until the year to which they apply. The Tax Courts have often overruled this law; and now it appears that the IRS may change its rules, allowing any prepayments if they extend no more than twelve months.

If a substantial tax break is at stake here, I suggest that you discuss this with your accountant.

Expense category: Varies depending on actual expenses.

Prizes

Prizes to customers and suppliers are deductible.
Expense category: Advertising; or Other expenses.

Prizes given to employees come under the same rules covered in **Awards**.

Product Development

Product development expenses are usually deductible, and may also be eligible for special tax credits (see **Tax Credits**).

Some development expenses that will benefit future years may have to be capitalized, and deducted over a period of at least five years. You should discuss these expenses with your accountant.

Expense category: Other expenses.

Professional Associations
Professional Organizations

Dues and meetings are deductible.

Expense category: Other expenses.

If part of your dues to a trade or professional association are for political lobbying, that portion of the dues is not deductible.

Professional Services and Publications

Professional, legal, and accounting services and publications are deductible.

Expense category: Legal and professional services. Office expense.

Taxes have a negative impact on taxpayers.
—Martin Regalia, vice president, U.S. Chamber of Commerce,
speaking before the House Committee on Small Business.

Profit Sharing Plans

Corporate profit sharing plans are deductible.

There is also something called a profit sharing plan that is really a Keogh retirement plan. See **Retirement Plans**.

Expense category: Pension and profit sharing plans.

Promissory Notes

A promissory note is a promise to pay money you owe, basically a loan agreement. The promissory note itself is not deductible, but the interest is.

Expense category: Interest (for the interest only).

Promotion

Promotional expenses are deductible. These may include free handouts, samples, news releases, audio and video productions, brochures, premiums, small gifts, greeting cards, or some service, performance or show.

Sometimes there may be a fine line between what is "promotion" and what is "entertainment." Promotion expenses are fully deductible, and entertainment is limited to a 50% deduction. The wise taxpayer carefully defines the expenses.

Expense category: Advertising; or Other expenses.

This agency intends to become an efficient consumer service organization, keeping taxpayers satisfied.

—IRS press release

Property Taxes

Payments for current year's property taxes are deductible. If you prepay property taxes (for next year), the full payment may or may not be deductible. See **Prepayments**.

In some cases, you can choose to capitalize real estate property taxes instead of writing them off. "Capitalize" means that you add the taxes to the cost of the real estate and depreciate them along with the real estate. This will result in a smaller write off currently, a larger write off in future years. If you choose to capitalize the property taxes (which in truth very few businesses do), I suggest you talk to your accountant about the methods and options.

Some states and localities also impose a property tax on business assets such as equipment, furniture and tools. This is known as a personal property tax—although the property is not personal property, it is business property. For this tax law, the word personal refers to property that is not real estate. The personal property tax could be quite high if your assets are assessed at a high value. Examine the tax bill, make sure retired or sold assets are not included, and that older assets are not overvalued. Personal property taxes are deductible.

Some states impose a property tax on inventory, called an inventory tax or a floor tax. This tax is deductible.

Expense category: Taxes and licenses.

Home-Based Businesses: You can deduct a percentage of your home property taxes only if you are allowed a home office deduction. See **Home Office.** Use Form 8829, "Expenses for Business Use of Your Home."

Real Estate Developers: If you purchase land that you plan to build on and sell, the property taxes are not currently deductible. The taxes must be capitalized.

There are four things that hold back human progress: Ignorance, stupidity, committees, and accountants.

—B. Bear, Owner, Pinball Alley, Willits, Ca.

Protective Gear

Deductible. Cost of cleaning is also deductible.
Expense category: Supplies.

Publications

Books, magazines, newsletters, newspapers, and all other business related publications are deductible.
Expense category: Office expense.

Punitive Damages

Punitive damages imposed by a government agency for breaking the law are not deductible. Any other punitive damages (such as for breach of contract), late charges, and the like, are deductible.

Expense category: Other expenses.

The National Commission on Restructuring the Internal Revenue Service, a joint House-Senate Congressional committee, after a year studying the IRS, recommended simplification of the tax laws as the key to a more "user friendly" IRS. Since the Commission's call for tax simplification was followed almost immediately by one of the most complex pieces of tax legislation in history, it was not clear how seriously its recommendations would be taken.

—Reported in the Washington Post

Raw Materials

Raw materials is a manufacturing term for the parts that go into whatever is being manufactured. Raw materials are inventory, and cannot be deducted until sold. See **Inventory**.

Expense category: Cost of goods sold.

Razing a Building

The cost to demolish a building must be added to the cost basis of the land. It cannot be deducted.

Real Estate

Real estate is buildings and land. Buildings can be depreciated. Land cannot be written off until sold. See **Buildings. Depreciation. Land.**

Expense category: Depreciation (for buildings). You must also fill out Form 4562, "Depreciation and Amortization."

Real Estate Taxes

Deductible. But see **Property Taxes**.

Expense category: Taxes and licenses.

Who Gets Welfare, Item #222: Ocean Spray Corp. received $700,000 in taxpayers' money last year to advertise Cranapple Juice all over the world.
—Reported by the Boston Globe

Rebates

Rebates paid out, if legal, are deductible. Many states outlaw kick-backs and bribes, however, and some types of rebates may fall into this legal swamp. If rebates are outlawed in your state, they are not deductible on your federal return, even if there is no federal law outlawing the expenditure. State law controls the deductibility.

Rebates received are not income; they are tax-free price reductions.

Also, see **Refunds**.

Expense category: Depends on how the money is actually spent.

Recreation Facilities

Recreation and athletic facilities on the business premises which are open to all employees are deductible. Recreation equipment can be deducted the year of purchase (up to a maximum amount) or depreciated. Structures and built-in structural components will have to be depreciated. See **Business Assets** and **Depreciation**.

Recreation facilities located away from the business premises (the company condo in Hawaii) may or may not be deductible. The IRS says there are restrictions, the Tax Courts disagree and say the facilities are deductible. If you own or lease such a facility, I suggest you talk to your accountant.

Expense category: Depreciation. You must also fill out Form 4562, "Depreciation and Amortization."

Dues and memberships paid to recreational clubs are not deductible.

Recreational Vehicles (RVs)

RVs used for business can be deducted or depreciated like other vehicles. See **Vehicles.** Keep in mind that all business deductions must meet the IRS's "ordinary" and "necessary" tests explained at the beginning of this book.

Expense category: The category "Car and truck expenses" is for all vehicle expenses except the cost of the vehicle itself, which is deducted or depreciated under "Depreciation." You must also file Form 4562, "Depreciation and Amortization."

If you drive a car, I'll tax the street
If you try to sit, I'll tax your seat
If you get too cold, I'll tax the heat
If you take a walk, I'll tax your feet.

—George Harrison, "Taxman" (The Beatles)

Referrals

Commissions or fees paid for referrals are deductible.
Expense category: Commissions and fees.

Commissions paid to acquire new customers who sign long term contracts, may have to be capitalized, and deducted over a period of years. The IRS says the deduction must be spread over the average number of years new customers stay with the business. This is something you should ask your accountant about.

Refunds

Money you refund to a customer is deductible. On the tax return, these sales refunds are shown in the income section, as a reduction to income, rather than in the expense section.
Expense category: Returns and allowances.

Rehabilitation, Buildings

See **Renovations, Repairs.** Also see **Buildings** for information about The Rehabilitation Tax Credit.

There is something un-American about a tax system that cannot be understood by an intelligent American.
—Tax expert and Stanford University professor George Marotta

Reimbursements

Self employed individuals who get reimbursed by clients for out-of-pocket expenses usually include the reimbursements as part of total income, and deduct the expenses as regular business expenses.

When an employer reimburses an employee for out-of-pocket business expenses, the employer is entitled to a tax deduction for the expenses. The reimbursement is not part of the employee's wages, is not subject to payroll taxes, and is not included on the employee's year end W-2 wage statement.

If the employer's reimbursement exceeds the employee's actual expenses, the excess is considered additional wages, deductible as payroll, and subject to payroll taxes.

If the employee does not receive a reimbursement or receives a reimbursement less than the actual expenses, the employee can take a partial (not full) itemized deduction on his or her 1040 tax return.

It is important to understand that the employer can get a full tax deduction by reimbursing the employee. The employee, if not reimbursed, cannot get a full tax deduction. Remember also that a self-employed individual—a sole proprietor, partner, or owner of a limited liability company—is not an employee of the business.

Expense category: Depends on how the money is actually spent.

Renovations

Building renovations that add to the value or extend the useful life of the building must be added to the cost of the building and depreciated. See **Depreciation**. Minor renovations and repairs can be deducted currently.

Expense category: Maintenance and repairs; or Depreciation (you must also fill out Form 4562, "Depreciation and Amortization").

Home-based businesses: Renovations to a home office are deductible only if you meet the home-office requirements. See **Home Office.** Reported on Form 8829, "Expenses for Business Use of Your Home."

Also see **Buildings** for information about the Rehabilitation Tax Credit and the Disabled Access Credit.

Who does their own business taxes? Why would you do that? I don't even do my personal taxes, and they would probably take thirty seconds.
—Unidentified New Jersey advertising executive, Inc. Magazine

---

Rent

Business rentals and leases—buildings, vehicles, equipment— are deductible (but see **Automobile Leases** below).

If you prepay rent (for part of the next year), the full payment may or may not be deductible. See **Prepayments**.

Expense category: Rent or lease.

Home-based Businesses: Rent on a home business is deductible only if you meet the home-office requirements. See **Home Office**. All home-office deductions are reported on Form 8829, "Expenses for Business Use of Your Home."

Automobile leases: Automobile leases, if 30 days or longer, are not 100% deductible. The IRS has a table, called "Inclusion Amounts for Cars," that shows how much of an auto lease can and cannot be deducted. See IRS Publication 463 for the table. This rules does not apply to trucks, vans or heavy sport utility vehicles.

Renting equipment from employees: Payments to employees for use of their equipment are considered taxable wages, not lease payments, unless the payments are part of a formal accountable plan. You should talk to an experienced accountant about this.

Rental Businesses

Businesses that rent out equipment can deduct or depreciate the equipment just like other depreciable business assets. Video stores can either write off videotapes when purchased (within certain limits) or depreciate them. See **Business Assets** and **Depreciation**.

Expense category: Depreciation. You must also fill out Form 4562, "Depreciation and Amortization."

Repairs

Repairs on business property or equipment are fully deductible as a current expense. However, major repairs or structural changes that add to the value or extend the useful life of an asset must be treated as a permanent investment and depreciated or deducted in the same manner as the purchase of a depreciable asset. See: **Business Assets, Depreciation**.

Expense category: Repairs and maintenance; or Depreciation (also file Form 4562, "Depreciation and Amortization").

I give all the papers to my tax accountant and just say, "Here." I pay a lot of money for that privilege.
  —Unidentified New York management consultant, Inc. Magazine

---

Research

Research expenses (Research and Development—R&D; Research and Experimentation—R&E) are usually deductible, and may also be eligible for special tax credits (see **Tax Credits**).

Some research expenses that will benefit future years may have to be capitalized, and deducted over a period of at least five years. You should discuss these expenses with your accountant.

What is a research expense? The term can be defined broadly but usually refers to developing, testing, refining, or improving a product or service. The Tax Court has ruled that software development may be considered a research expense, eligible for the tax credit; the IRS disagrees, so I suggest you check with your accountant.

Expense category: Other expenses.

Reserves for Bad Debts

Reserves for bad debts, funds set aside in anticipation of bad debts, are not deductible. Actual bad debts are deductible. See **Bad Debts.**

Reserves for Self Insurance

Reserves for self insurance, funds set aside in anticipation of having a claim that might otherwise be covered by insurance, are not deductible. If you have a loss, you may then have a deduction. See **Casualty Losses.**

Restaurant and Bar "Smallware"

Glasses, plates, utensils, bar supplies and the like are deductible. However, if the "smallware" was purchased before starting the business, the cost must be depreciated.

Expense Category: Supplies.

Restoration

The cost of restoring or reconditioning property, if it adds to the value or extends the life of the property, must be added to the cost of the property and deducted or depreciated along with the property. See **Business Assets** and **Depreciation**. If, however, the money spent on restoration is not significant, the expenses can be deducted the year incurred.

Expense category: Repairs and maintenance; or Depreciation (you must also fill out Form 4562, "Depreciation and Amortization").

The rich are there to make all the money and pay none of the taxes. The middle class are there to do all the work and pay all the taxes. The poor are there to scare the daylights out of the middle class so they'll keep working and paying the taxes.

—George Carlin

Retirement Plans

You may invest a portion of your profit in a special tax-deferred retirement plan and pay no income taxes on the money invested or the interest earned until you retire and withdraw the funds.

There are several tax-deferred retirement plans available to business owners and their employees. Each plan has different options, different contributions, different deadlines for making contributions, and, most important to employers, different requirements for including your employees in the plans. You can choose just one plan, or you may be able to set up multiple plans.

Retirement contributions an employer makes on behalf of employees are deductible. Retirement contributions a business owner makes for himself may or may not be deductible, depending on many factors.

The different retirement plans include:

1. Individual Retirement Account (IRA).
2. Roth IRA, a different kind of IRA (named after Senator Roth, who sponsored the legislation).
3. Self Employed Pension Plan (SEP or SEP-IRA).

4. Keogh Plan, also called HR-10 Plan (named after Congressman Keogh and his bill number).

5. Deferred Compensation Plan, more commonly called a 401(k) Plan (named after the IRS Code section number).

6. Savings Incentive Match Plan for Employees (SIMPLE).

7. Corporate Retirement Plan, also known as an ERISA Plan (Employee Retirement Income Security Act).

Talk to your accountant about the different plans, and which plan will best suit your own needs, your budget, and your employees. Banks and insurance companies offer all of the retirement plans, and can provide you with full details about each plan. Also see IRS Publication 590, "Individual Retirement Arrangements" and Publication 560, "Retirement Plans for the Small Business."

Expense category: Deducted on Form 1040.

After paying my Social Security, Medicare, and federal and state income taxes, my wife and I could finally use my $10,000 first year's income to splurge on food and housing. Three years later, after working 80-hour weeks without a single vacation, I reluctantly added an employee. I quickly discovered I was to become the employee's "mother," legally required to pay worker's compensation, unemployment and disability insurance for him, as well as paying for his Social Security and Medicare benefits. I quickly found out how badly the government penalizes anyone trying to make a decent (i.e. subsistence) living.

—Business owner Scott Grimshaw, writing in Nation's Business

Returned Checks

A genteel term for bounced (bad) checks. Bounced checks are deductible as a bad debt expense. See **Bounced Checks. Bad Debts.**

Expense category: Bad debts.

Returned Goods

Refunds on returned goods are deducted from your income in figuring your taxes. See **Refunds.** There is no additional deduction for returned goods. The goods should be added back into inventory if they are still salable, or left off the inventory if they are unsalable. At the end of the year, the returned goods become part of your inventory and cost-of-goods-sold calculations. See **Inventory**.

Expense category: Returns and allowances.

When my partner and I asked the city of Grand Rapids what was needed to open a business, we were told we needed only two things: a business license and a sales tax license. We obtained the licenses and opened a downtown flea market. We advertised our grand opening by offering brand-name nail polish for 25¢ as well as a package of noodles for 25¢.

On opening day we got nailed by city licensing for not having a license to sell paint (nail polish), by grocer licensing for not having a day-old variance, and by the fire marshall for not having $900 in fire extinguishers. Two men showed up and demanded to inspect the freight elevator, which hadn't run since 1935. Inspection fee: $285. We were deluged with forms for business activity taxes, interim business taxes and inventory taxes.

When we hired a woman to mind the store, we got this huge form from the unemployment office that looked like a wallpaper sample book.

There were just the two of us. We closed our business forever. One week later we were cited for failure to get a going-out-of-business license. A week after that, the mayor appeared on TV saying, "We have to seek new ways to attract business to downtown Grand Rapids."

—Jim McFeely, commenting in Inc. Magazine

Rewards

Rewards to customers, vendors, and other non-employees are deductible.

Rewards to employees are also deductible. Rewards up to $400 to employees are tax-free to the employees. But rewards above $400 are taxable to the employees as part of their regular wages, and subject to regular payroll taxes.

Expense category: Advertising, or Other Expenses (rewards to non-employees); Employee benefit programs, or Wages (rewards to employees).

Roads

You can deduct the costs of maintaining a private road or driveway on your business property. The cost of constructing a road must be depreciated. See **Depreciation.**

Expense category: Repairs and maintenance; or Depreciation (you must also fill out Form 4562, "Depreciation and Amortization").

Robbery Losses

Deductible, but with special rules. See **Casualty Losses.**

Royalties

Royalties you pay are deductible.
Expense category: Commissions and fees.

Print neatly.

—*"Dynamic Tax Tip" from the Internal Revenue Service*

Safe Deposit Box

Safe deposit boxes are deductible.
Expense category: Office expense.

Safety Equipment

Safety equipment, first aid kits, fire extinguishers, and the like are deductible. Large structural safety equipment may have to be added to the cost of the building and depreciated. See **Depreciation.**

Expense category: Supplies; or Depreciation (you must also fill out Form 4562, "Depreciation and Amortization").

Salaries

Employee salaries are deductible. See **Payroll.**
Expense category: Wages.

Sales Refunds

Money you refund to a customer is deductible. On your tax return, these sales refunds are shown in the income section, as a reduction to income, rather than in the expense section.

Expense category: Returns and allowances.

Sales Returns

Refunds on returned goods are deducted from your income in figuring your taxes. See **Refunds**. There is no additional deduction for returned goods. The goods should be added back into inventory if they are still salable, or left off the inventory if they are unsalable. At the end of the year, the returned goods become part of your inventory and cost-of-goods-sold calculations. See **Inventory**.

Expense category: Returns and allowances.

Sales Tax

Sales tax paid on business equipment, depreciable assets, and vehicles, should be added to the cost of the equipment, and deducted or depreciated. See **Business Assets** and **Depreciation**. Do not deduct the sales tax separately.

Sales tax paid on supplies and similar purchases should be added to the cost of the goods or services purchased, and deducted. Again, do not deduct the sales tax separately.

Sales tax collected from your customers: Most businesses include sales tax in gross income, and deduct it as a business expense. Net effect is zero.

Expense category: Taxes and licenses (for sales tax collected from customers and remitted to the government).

Who Gets Welfare, First Prize: General Motors received more than $110.6 million in taxpayers' money in federal subsidies, specifically to create jobs. General Motors earned $4.7 billion in profits. During that period, General Motors laid off 104,000 workers, 25% of their U.S. work force.

—Reported by the Women's International League, Philadelphia

Samples

Samples of your merchandise, given to prospective buyers or to people who might review or publicize your products, are deductible. You deduct the cost of the samples (not the retail or market value) as part of cost-of-goods-sold. See **Inventory**.

Expense category: Cost of goods sold.

Scholarships

Scholarships given to employees are deductible. See **Education Expenses**. Scholarships given to an employee's spouse or children are usually considered taxable wages, but there are some exceptions. You should ask your accountant about this.

Scholarships given to members of the community as a gesture of goodwill may be deductible as a promotional expense. Again, check with your accountant.

SECA Tax

SECA stands for Self Employment Contributions Act, and refers to the self-employment tax. See **Self Employment Tax**. It is not deductible.

Many women tell me, "I'd rather pay more taxes than risk an audit." I never hear it from men. This is clearly a problem.
—Enrolled Agent and tax advisor Jan Zobel, Oakland, Ca.

Section 179 Deduction

This refers to the tax law that allows a business to fully deduct some assets the year of purchase rather than depreciate them over several years. See **Business Assets**.

Expense category: Depreciation. You must also fill out Form 4562, "Depreciation and Amortization."

Security

Security services and patrols are deductible. Permanent and built-in security systems may have to be depreciated. See **Business Assets** and **Depreciation.**

Expense category: Other expenses; or Office expense; or (for permanent built-in systems) Depreciation (you must also fill out Form 4562, "Depreciation and Amortization").

Self Employment Tax

Self-employment tax, also known as SECA (Self Employment Contributions Act), is combined Social Security and Medicare tax for self-employed individuals. Sole proprietors, partners in partnerships, and active owners of limited liability companies are subject to self-employment tax. The tax is not imposed on owners (shareholders) of small corporations, who are employee of the business and pay regular employee payroll taxes.

You cannot deduct self-employment tax as a business expense. However, you are allowed a tax deduction on your personal 1040 return. You reduce your total taxable income by one-half of the self-employment tax you pay.

For more information, see IRS Publication #533, "Information on Self-Employment Tax."

Expense category: Taken on Form 1040.

Your Tax Dollars At Work: The U.S. General Services Administration (GSA) is paying $17 million a year rent on an empty office building in Washington D.C., which was to house the Federal Communications Commission (FCC) offices. The FCC administrators have refused to move to the building, which is in Southwest D.C. a long distance from other government offices. The building is half-owned by Franklin Henry, a close friend Al Gore. The Justice Department and a House committee are investigating whether the $400 million dollar lease involved illegal or improper actions. The GSA denies the allegations. —Reported in Business Week

---

Just be glad you aren't getting all the government you're paying for.
—Will Rogers

Self Insurance

Self insurance is not really insurance at all, because no insurance policy is purchased. Not deductible.

Employers: Instead of (or in addition to) buying health insurance for your employees, you can pay their medical bills, or reimburse them for their medical bills, and get a full deduction. For more information see **Health Insurance**.
Expense category: Employee benefit programs.

Seminars

Most business seminars are deductible, but see **Education**.
Expense category: Other expenses.

SEP / SEP-IRA

SEP stands for Simplified Employee Pension plan, a tax deferred retirement plan. Also known as SEP-IRA. See **Retirement Plans**.
Expense category: Deducted on Form 1040.

Service Contracts

Service contracts and extended warranties are usually deductible. However, see **Prepayments**.
Expense category: Other expenses.

Service Mark

A service mark is a trademark that applies to a service (trademarks apply to goods). Service marks must be amortized (deducted) over a fifteen year period. See **Depreciation**.
Expense category: Depreciation. (Also fill out IRS Form #4562).

Sewer Service

Sewer charges are deductible. Sewer assessments, if for construction of new sewers, sometimes must be added to the cost of the building and depreciated as part of the building. See **Depreciation.**

Expense category: Utilities; or Depreciation (you must also fill out Form 4562, "Depreciation and Amortization").

Home-Based Businesses: You can deduct a percentage of your home utilities only if you are allowed a home office deduction. See **Home Office.** Home-office utilities are reported on Form 8829, "Expenses for Business Use of Your Home."

Manufacturers: Sewer service for the manufacturing process may have to be added to the cost of the inventory rather than being written off immediately. See **Inventory.**

The farmer is the man, The farmer is the man,
He lives on his credit until fall.
Well, his pants are wearin' thin, His condition is a sin,
But the taxes on the farmer feeds us all.
　　　—Taxes on the Farmer Feeds Us All, song from the Depression,
　　　　　author unknown (as sung by Ry Cooder).

Shipping

Deductible, with some limitations. see **Freight.**
Expense category: Other expenses.

Shipping Supplies

Shipping supplies are deductible unless they are an integral part of the product you are shipping. Then they must be included as part of inventory. See **Inventory.**

Expense category: Supplies (if deductible currently); or Cost of goods sold (if included in inventory).

Shoplifting Losses

Shoplifting losses are deductible as part of cost-of-goods-sold. See **Inventory**.

Showroom

The cost of renting a showroom is deductible. The cost of a building (or part of a building) you own can be depreciated. See **Buildings**. The cost of a home-based showroom is deductible only if you meet the home office requirements. See **Home Office**.

Expense category: Rent or lease (for rented space); Depreciation (owned building); Form 8829, "Expenses for Business Use of Your Home" (for home based businesses).

Shows

Shows you put on to promote your business are deductible. Food and beverages served are fully deductible. Shows you attend are also deductible, although meals you purchase are only 50% deductible.

Expense category: Advertising. Other expenses. Meals.

Sick Pay

Employee sick pay is deductible. It is considered regular, taxable wages.

Expense category: Wages.

Self-employed individuals (sole proprietors, partners in partnerships, and members of limited liability companies) cannot deduct their own sick pay, because they are not legally employees of their businesses. See **Draw** and **Paying Yourself**.

Signs

Most signs can, at your option, be deducted the year of purchase or depreciated. Large and expensive outdoor signs, however, are considered land improvements, and must be depreciated. See **Business Assets** and **Depreciation**.

Without computers, the government would be unable to function at the level of effectiveness and efficiency that we have come to expect. This is because the primary function of the government is—and here I am quoting directly from the U.S. Constitution—to "spew out paper." This can be very time consuming if you use the old fashioned method of having human beings sit down and think about what each piece of paper is actually going to say. This is why today's government uses computers, which are capable of cranking out millions of documents per day, thereby freeing government employees for more important responsibilities, such as not answering their phones. —Dave Barry, Home Office Computing magazine

SIMPLE Plan

SIMPLE stands for Savings Incentive Match Plan for Employees, a tax deferred retirement plan. See **Retirement Plans**.

Expense category: Deducted on Form 1040.

Simplified Employee Pension Plan

A tax deferred retirement plan. Also known as a SEP or SEP-IRA. See **Retirement Plans**.

Expense category: Deducted on Form 1040.

"Smallware" for Restaurants and Bars

Deductible, but see **Restaurant and Bar Smallware**.

Snacks

I looked this one up. Nowhere in the IRS Code does it mention snacks or say whether snacks are deductible. (The peanuts *are* salty.) The IRS does allow a deduction for expenses that are ordinary and necessary. (The root beer is cold.) And everybody knows that snacks are ordinary and necessary. Absolutely. (We're out of potato chips. Do we get to deduct the mileage driving to the store to get more?)

Expense category: Office expense.

Your Tax Dollars At Work: Government travel costs taxpayers more than $3 billion a year. In a recent Office of Management and Budget (OMB) investigation, government bureaucrats could not produce a reason for 27% of their trips. U.S. General Services Administration (GSA) auditors say it's a common practice for government employees to disguise personal travel as business. —*Reported in the Baltimore Sun*

Spouse

You can hire your spouse as an employee of your business, and get a full deduction like you would for any other employee. As an employee, a spouse is subject to all regular employee withholding and payroll taxes except for Federal Unemployment (FUTA) taxes. (The FUTA exemption does not apply to corporations).

Expense category: Wages.

If you employ your spouse, officially on the payroll and doing legitimate work, he or she is eligible for the same 100% deductible health benefits offered to all your employees. In fact, if you employ your spouse, you also get 100% deductible coverage for yourself, instead of the 70%. See page 106, **Family Employees**, for a full explanation of this deduction.

Expense category: Employee benefit programs.

Business Expenses: Any business expenses your spouse incurs can be deducted only if your spouse is an official employee of your business, or if your spouse is a partner in the business.

Expense category: Varies depending on actual expenses.

IRS definition: A spouse is a legally married wife or husband. No deductions are allowed for domestic partners or for same-sex spouses.

Social Security Tax

Social Security and Medicare are the two combined payroll taxes deducted from every employee's paycheck and collected from every employer. This pair of taxes is often called FICA (Federal Insurance Contributions Act), or OASDI (Old Age, Survivors and Disability Insurance), or simply Social Security.

The employer's portion of the tax is deductible. That is, the tax that you as an employer pay on behalf of your employees can be deducted on your tax return.

Expense category: Taxes and licenses.

All self-employed people also pay a combined Social Security and Medicare tax; it's called self employment tax. It is not deductible, though you are allowed a tax deduction for part of it on the 1040 return. See **Self Employment Tax**.

Give me a list of write-offs organized by type of deduction, and you're guaranteed to knock half off your tax preparation bill.
—*CPA Andrew Blackman, New York City*

Software

Computer software that you purchase can be depreciated over three years, or less if the software has a shorter life (such as a tax program, which is only good for one year).

Software that was packaged with your computer when you bought it is considered part of the cost of the computer.

If you develop software programs, you can, at your option, write off the development costs as current expenses. You also have the option to depreciate software development costs over five years. See **Depreciation**.

The Tax Court has ruled that software development may be considered a research expense, eligible for the Research Tax Credit (see **Tax Credits**). The IRS disagrees. Check with your accountant.

The IRS says that software is an intangible, and therefore not eligible for the Sec. 179 First Year Write-Off of business assets.

Expense category: Office expense (if a minor cost); Other expenses (development costs); or Depreciation (you must also fill out Form 4562, "Depreciation and Amortization").

"MOST PEOPLE BRING THEIR ACCOUNTANT!'"

Standard Meal Allowance

You are allowed a 50% deduction for meals while travelling away from home overnight on business. You can keep track of actual meal expenses, or you may be able to use a per diem standard meal allowance. IRS Publication 1542, "Per Diem Rates," shows the current per diem rates for different cities.

The IRS has said that only corporations can use the per diem rates for meals, but the Tax Court has ruled otherwise. If you want to use the per diem rates, check with your accountant first.

Expense category: Meals and entertainment.

Standard Mileage Allowance (Rate)

The IRS has a standard mileage allowance deduction (standard mileage rate) for every business mile driven. This allowance is in lieu of actual vehicle expenses such as gas, oil changes, maintenance, and the cost of the vehicle. The 2002 rate is 36½¢ per mile. There are restrictions and fine-print rules. See **Vehicles**.

Expense category: Car and truck expenses.

The hardest thing in the world to understand is income tax.

—*Albert Einstein*

There are billions there in corporate loopholes. $23 billion in last fall's appropriations bill. Practically every bit was pork. I proposed a commission on corporate welfare. It didn't get through the House.

—Senator John McCain

Start-Up Costs

Business expenses incurred before you start your business (called start-up expenses, though they are really pre-start-up expenses) come under two different tax rules.

General preliminary costs incurred before you actually pick a specific business, such as investigating different business possibilities, are usually not deductible at all. The IRS considers these personal expenses, no tax write-off ever.

Once you've decided on a particular business, the start-up expenses (not including the general preliminary costs mentioned above) are deductible, but not 100% the year you incur them. You have the option to capitalize them, which means no deduction at all until you quit or sell your business; or to deduct them ("amortize" them) over a 60-month period, or longer if you prefer, starting the month the business begins operation. "Amortize" is an accounting term for writing off intangible assets over a period of years.

To figure your deduction, divide your total start-up costs by the number of months in the write-off period (at least 60, but more if you want to spread the tax deduction over a longer period). The result is the amount you can deduct each month. To get this amortization option, you must start taking the deduction the first year you are in business. Otherwise, you lose the option and will be required to capitalize the start-up expenses.

Start-up expenses are a real sore spot for new businesses, because the expenses include any and all business expenditures incurred before you are open for business. They include organizational expenses, such as hiring an accountant or a lawyer to draft up legal documents; and even conventional pre-opening expenses such as rent, telephone, advertising, stationery, etc.

The IRS has often wrangled with taxpayers over which costs are and aren't "start-up," and at what point a new venture is actually "in business." The IRS has stated that a business hasn't actually started until it produces income. Tax Courts have disagreed and have ruled that once a business is set up and "open for business," that is, trying to generate income, it is officially started even if it has not made a sale yet. This is an area to discuss with an accountant. I suggest you put off as many expenses as possible until after the business is operating.

One way around some of the start-up expense problems is to start your business at home if that's feasible, just as small an operation as possible to meet IRS requirements. Once you have generated a little income, *then* spend your money on finding a new location, on stationery, furniture and equipment, and on accounting and legal advice. Since you are now officially in business, the expenses are deductible as regular business expenses, no longer subject to the start-up rules.

If you do incur start-up expenses but never actually start a business, the expenses may, in some situations, be deductible as a capital loss under the IRS's capital gains and loss rules.

Americans have the impression that understanding the tax laws will only serve to increase the amount of taxes they must pay.
—Mike Mares, American Institute of Certified Public Accountants (AICPA), Washington DC

State Taxes

The list of state taxes on businesses is virtually endless. Property taxes, income taxes and sales taxes are the most common. Many states tax the manufacturers, wholesalers and retailers of alcoholic beverages, fuels, tobacco, motor vehicles and airplanes. Most states tax mining, logging, and real estate dealings. Many states have an admissions tax on theaters, amusement parks, etc. Many states tax freight companies. Several states tax forest land. Some states have a chain store tax for businesses with more than one location. Some states tax hotel rooms and restaurant meals. Some states have state business licenses and annual fees (often called a "business privilege tax").

All these taxes are deductible.

Expense category: Taxes and licenses.

Former Senator William Proxmire, famous for his Golden Fleece awards, uncovered these taxpayer-financed grants:

$500,000 grant to measure aggression by counting the number of times monkeys bit on a rubber hose when given electric shocks.

$104,000 research project entitled "The Peruvian Brothels as Sexual Dispensary and Social Arena."

$86,000 expedition to the Himalayas to learn why the advent of mountaineering as an economic enterprise has brought a return to more orthodox religious practices.

$7,500 project to find out if drunk fish are more aggressive than sober fish.

$2,500 study proving that fat people prefer to eat at all-you-can-eat smorgasbords.

$6,000 study on the effects of marijuana on scuba divers (it gets them stoned).

$3,000 study on the use of umbrellas.

$51,900 study to prove that people become mad when their personal space is violated.

$120,100 project to develop a motorcycle that steers backwards.

$90,000 grant to study "Behavioral Determinants of Vegetarianism."

$75,000 grant to research the causes of smiling by bowlers, hockey players and pedestrians.

$360,000 study to determine the average speed of trucks in New York City.

The average taxpayer worked a record 129 days last year, or until May 9, to earn enough money to pay his or her combined federal, state, and local tax bill. —The Tax Foundation, Washington D.C.

Federal, state and local taxes now take 36% of the average worker's income. —Jerry J. Jasinowski, President, National Association of Manufacturers

Stationery

Stationery, envelopes, and other office supplies can be deducted.
Expense category: Office expense.

Stereo System

The office stereo system can be deducted or depreciated, as long as it is not, to quote the IRS, "lavish or extravagant under the circumstances." See **Business Assets** and **Depreciation**. The cost of CDs, tapes and albums is deductible.

Expense category: Depreciation. Also file Form 4562, "Depreciation and Amortization." Office expense (CDs and tapes).

Stock

Shares of corporate stock (stock certificates) that you purchase are usually not deductible as a business expense.

If you are buying a business—acquiring the corporate stock of a corporation you are buying—you may be able to deduct some of the cost. It is very important to talk to your accountant before making such a purchase. A lot of tax money may be at stake, depending on how the purchase is legally structured.

Cost of issuing your own corporate stock may have to be amortized over a period of years. This is also an area you should discuss with an accountant.

The term "stock" is also used to describe inventory, goods for sale. See **Inventory**.

Livestock on farms may or may not be deductible depending on many factors.

In this world, nothing is certain but death and taxes.
—Benjamin Franklin, 1789

The main difference between death and taxes is that taxes get worse every time Congress meets. —Will Rogers

Death and taxes are certain, but death isn't an annual event.
—B. Bear, Owner, Pinball Alley, Willits, Ca.

Stolen Property

Stolen depreciable property (business assets that you are depreciating) can be deducted as a casualty loss, but only to the extent of the undepreciated balance. If you deducted the entire asset the first year, you have no deductible loss.

Inventory that is stolen is deducted as part of your cost-of-goods-sold. See **Inventory**.

If stolen property was covered by insurance, you are not allowed a deduction for the loss (since you did not really incur a loss).

Expense category: Depends on what kind of property was stolen. You also must fill out Form 4684, "Casualties and Thefts."

Storage Costs
Storage Facilities

Storage costs are deductible. Rent of a storage facility is deductible.

Expense category: Rent or Lease, for the rental fees. Other Expenses for the incidental costs.

Storage facilities you own can be depreciated or, for some buildings, can be written off the year of purchase. See **Depreciation**.

77% of small businesses polled think the existing tax system should be scrapped. —*National Small Business United/Arthur Anderson Study*

Store

The cost of renting a store is deductible. The cost of a building (or part of a building) you own can be depreciated. See **Buildings**. The cost of a home-based store is deductible if you meet the home office requirements. See **Home Office**.

Expense category: Rent or lease (for rented space); Depreciation (owned building); Form 8829, "Expenses for Business Use of Your Home" (for home based businesses).

Store Fixtures

Store fixtures can be deducted or depreciated. See **Business Assets. Depreciation.** Built-in fixtures that become part of a building may have to be depreciated along with the structure. See **Buildings**.

Expense category: Depreciation. You must also fill out Form 4562, "Depreciation and Amortization."

Storm Losses

Deductible. See **Casualty Losses**.

Expense category: Depends on kind of property lost, damaged or destroyed. You also must fill out Form 4684, "Casualties and Thefts."

Structures

Buildings you own must be depreciated. See **Buildings. Depreciation.** Rental on buildings is deductible.

Expense category: Rent or lease; or Depreciation (you must also fill out Form 4562, "Depreciation and Amortization").

Home based businesses: The cost of a structure is deductible only if you meet the home office requirements. See **Home Office.** All home-office expenses are reported on Form 8829, "Expenses for Business Use of Your Home."

Washington, D.C.: An $800 million U.S. Postal Service marketing and advertising program was outlined Thursday by Chief Marketing Officer Allen R. Kane at a Washington press breakfast. According to Kane, the marketing and ad budget is $150 million more than last year, when his predecessor, Loren Smith, was forced to resign for overspending the previous $150 million marketing and advertising budget.

—Reported in Direct Marketing News

Studio

The cost of renting a studio is deductible. The cost of a building (or part of a building) you own must be depreciated. See **Buildings**.

Expense category: Rent or lease (for rented space); Depreciation, and you must also fill out Form 4562, "Depreciation and Amortization" (owned building).

Home based businesses: The cost of a structure is deductible only if you meet the home office requirements. See **Home Office**. All home-office expenses are reported on Form 8829, "Expenses for Business Use of Your Home."

Subcontractors

Subcontractors are usually considered independent contractors,

in business for themselves. Their fees are deductible. See **Independent Contractors.**
Expense category: Commissions and fees.

If a subcontractor is constructing or doing major repairs or renovations on a building, the subcontractor's fees may have to be added to the cost of the building, and depreciated. See **Depreciation**.
Expense category: Depreciation. You must also fill out Form 4562, "Depreciation and Amortization."

Subscriptions

Subscriptions are deductible.
Expense category: Office expense.

"You have reached the Internal Revenue Service. Due to the high volume of calls currently in our system, our representatives are unable to take your call." —Recorded response when calling the IRS help line, 1-800-TAX-1040.

Supplies

Office supplies are deductible. See **Office Supplies.**
Manufacturing supplies must be added to the cost of the goods being manufactured, and included in inventory. See **Inventory**.
Shipping supplies are deductible unless they are an integral part of the product you are shipping. Then they must be included as part of inventory. See **Inventory**.
Expense category: Supplies; or (if included in inventory) Cost of goods sold.

Surveys

The cost of conducting surveys is deductible.
Expense category: Legal and professional services.

Tariffs

Tariffs, customs fees and duties are deductible. Fees charged by customs brokers and international handlers are deductible. Instead of deducting tariffs immediately, in some cases the fees can be added to the cost of inventory and written off as cost of goods sold. You may want to ask your accountant about this.

Expense category: Commissions and fees. Taxes and licenses.

I have come to the conclusion that one useless man is called a disgrace, two are called a law firm, and three or more become a Congress.
—Founding Father John Adams

Tax Credits

Tax credits are special tax incentives created by Congress, to stimulate the economy or to encourage businesses to act in socially or environmentally responsible ways.

Tax credits should not be confused with tax deductions. A tax deduction is an item of expense that reduces your business profit. This book lists 422 tax deductions. A tax credit, by comparison, does not reduce your business profit. It reduces your taxes directly, dollar for dollar.

For example, a tax *deduction* of $100 may save you $30 or $40 in taxes, depending on your tax bracket. A tax *credit* of $100 will save you a full $100 in taxes, regardless of your tax bracket. Tax credits are a real gold mine.

Tax credits come and go, available one year and not the next. If you fail to take a tax credit you are entitled to, the IRS will not tell you. So you need to do your own research.

Last year there were tax credits for: buying electric vehicles; producing alcohol fuel; research; providing low-income housing; making your business more accessible to disabled people; producing electricity from renewable resources; hiring employees who meet certain eligibility requirements (the IRS has a list of types of employees who qualify); rehabilitating old buildings and historic structures; investing in certain "economically challenged" communities.

Some tax credits appear on partnership or corporation returns. Other credits are on the 1040 return. The IRS's Publication 334, *Tax Guide for Small Business* lists the current credits.

Tax Penalties

Tax penalties are not deductible.

Tax Return Preparation

Fees paid to prepare business tax returns are fully deductible. For sole proprietors, only the cost of preparing the business part of your 1040 tax return (schedule C or schedule C-EZ and related schedules) is deductible.

Expense category: Legal and professional services.

We would collect more money if we audited more returns, but I don't think anyone would want a tax system where the audit coverage was really very high. That would be a very intrusive, burdensome kind of system. If more people knew what a small percentage we actually audit, we'd have an enormous number of taxpayers playing audit roulette.

—Former IRS Commissioner Jerome Kurtz

Taxes

Most taxes other than Federal income tax and self employment tax are deductible. See the listings of specific taxes for more details.

Expense category: Taxes and licenses.

Telephone

All telephone services, fees and taxes are deductible.

Expense category: Office expense.

Home-Based Businesses: Tax deductions for a home telephone are limited. You may not deduct the basic monthly rate for the first telephone line into the home. Expenses beyond the basic rate, such as business-related long distance calls, optional services, Yellow Pages listings, and any special business equipment are deductible. Any additional business lines into the house after the first line are fully deductible if used exclusively for business.

For tax purposes, it does not matter to the IRS how the phone is listed, business or personal. The first line into your home is not deductible even if it is listed as a business phone, even if it is used 100% for business. A second line is fully deductible, regardless of its listing, as long as it is used 100% for business. Cellular phone service is also deductible.

Expense category: Office expense.

Congress today is more bought than it ever has been. Every night in Washington, there are five or six fundraisers to collect money from lobbyists. That's one reason we haven't been able to deal with the question of tax justice. The people who want preferences buy them with their tremendous campaign contributions.

—Former Representative Charles A. Vanik

Theft Losses

Stolen depreciable property (business assets that you are depreciating) can be deducted as a theft loss, but only to the extent of the undepreciated balance. If you wrote the entire asset off the first year, you have no deductible loss.

Inventory that is stolen is deducted as part of your cost-of-goods-sold. See **Inventory**.

If stolen property was covered by insurance, you are not allowed a deduction for the loss (since you did not really incur a loss).

For more information, see IRS Publication 547, "Casualties, Disasters, and Thefts."

Expense category: Depends on what kind of property was stolen. You also must fill out Form 4684, "Casualties and Thefts."

```
Latest Revision For:                          2002
1040  Individual Income Tax Return
      Department of the Treasury—Internal Revenue Service
Income    Please attach        |
          Copy B of your       | Your social security number
          Forms W–2 here.      |

1. How much money did
   you make last year?  . . . . . . . . . . ▶  [   ]

2. Send it in . . . . . . . . . . . . . . . . ▶  [   ]
```

This Book

That's right. The money you paid for this book is 100% deductible. In fact, you can deduct twice as much, just by going out and buying a second copy.

Expense category: Office expense.

And it came to pass in those days that there went out a decree from Caesar Augustus, that all the world should be taxed. This decree seems to have been enforced ever since.

—*Prof. C. Northcote Parkinson*

Tickets

Tickets to sporting, music, theater and similar events are considered entertainment. Only 50% of the cost can be deducted, and only if there is a valid business reason to buy the tickets. You should also be aware that this deduction is based on the face value of the ticket. If you paid a scalper or ticket broker $500 for a $35 Rolling Stones ticket, you only get to deduct 50% of the $35 face value.

If you buy tickets to give away to a client or prospect, the tickets are no longer entertainment expenses, they are gift expenses. The full cost, up to $25 per recipient per year, is deductible.

Raffle tickets are usually considered donations, and only corporations can deduct donations. Senator Ebenezer Scrooge himself must have put through this law.

Parking tickets and speeding tickets and other citations for illegal activities are not deductible.

Expense category: Meals and entertainment (if entertainment). Other expenses (if gift). Charitable contributions (if charitable).

Tips

(1) Don't invest in anything that eats; (2) Don't tell the IRS auditor that income taxes are unconstitutional; and (3) Don't waste your money on the lottery: your chance of winning is the same whether you buy a ticket or not.

Tips paid for meal service are considered part of the meal, and are only 50% deductible. Tips for services other than food are fully deductible.

Expense category: Meals and entertainment; or Other expenses.

The federal government will spend $1 billion over five years for anti-drug advertising. The money will go to the same advertising companies that routinely pocket billions of dollars for persuading people to smoke and drink. The $1 billion is part of the Office of National Drug Control Policy's annual $16.8 billion budget. Yes, you read that right: The War on Drugs costs taxpayers $16.8 billion every year.
　　　　　　　—David Armstrong, On Media, San Francisco Chronicle

The War on Drugs is a failure.　　　*—Former drug "czar" William Bennett*

Tolls

Vehicle tolls are deductible. If you take the standard mileage allowance, tolls are deductible in addition to the mileage allowance.

Expense category: Car and truck expenses.

Tools

Inexpensive tools and tools with a life of a year or less are deductible. More expensive tools can be deducted the year of purchase or depreciated. See **Business Assets. Depreciation.**

Expense category: Supplies (if low cost or short lived); or Depreciation (you must also fill out Form 4562, "Depreciation and Amortization").

Tractors

Tractors and construction equipment are deducted or depreciated like business assets. See **Business Assets** and **Depreciation**. They do not come under vehicle rules.

Expense category: Depreciation. You must also fill out Form 4562, "Depreciation and Amortization."

The truth is that we have such a limited budget, such limited manpower to enforce the income tax laws and collect the revenue, that the only way we can keep them honest and paying their taxes is to keep them afraid.
—Former IRS Commissioner Donald Alexander

Trade

Trade, as in exchange or barter, is a taxable transaction. Goods or services received in trade are deductible at their fair market value. See **Barter**.

Expense category: Depends on what is acquired in trade.

Trade Association

Dues and meetings are deductible.

Expense category: Other expenses.

If part of your dues to a trade or professional association are for political lobbying, that portion of the dues is not deductible.

Trade Dress

Trade dress is a form of trademark. The cost must be amortized (deducted) over a fifteen year period. See **Depreciation**.

Expense category: Depreciation. You must also fill out Form 4562, "Depreciation and Amortization."

Trade Name

Trade names are similar to trademarks. The cost must be amortized (deducted) over a fifteen year period. See **Depreciation**.

Expense category: Depreciation. You must also fill out Form 4562, "Depreciation and Amortization."

Doing taxes is not an effective use of a business owner's time.
—Jane Wesman., author and owner,
J. Wesman Public Relations

Trade Show

Admission fees to trade shows are deductible. Travel (with a few exceptions) and lodging are deductible. Meals are 50% deductible. See **Travel. Meals.**

Expense category: Other expenses (for the show itself). Travel.

Trademark

The cost of obtaining a trademark must be amortized (deducted) over a fifteen year period. See **Depreciation**.

Expense category: Depreciation. You must also fill out Form 4562, "Depreciation and Amortization."

If you acquire rights to a trademark from another business, under a licensing agreement, the payments are deductible when paid. They do not have to be amortized.

Expense category: Other expenses.

Trailers

Travel trailers, utility trailers, and movable, non-permanent mobile homes can be deducted or depreciated. See **Business Assets** and **Depreciation**.

Permanent mobile homes are usually considered real property, and must be depreciated accordingly. See **Mobile Home**.

Trailers are not considered vehicles, so they do not come under the restrictions the IRS imposes on vehicles.

Expense category: Depreciation. You must also fill out Form 4562, "Depreciation and Amortization."

Training

Training expenses, seminars, videos, manuals, etc. are deductible. But see **Education Expenses**.

Expense category: Other expenses.

Every year, Money magazine asks 50 different tax preparers to prepare a 1040 form for a sample family. No two preparers arrived at the same result.

—Reported by the Tax Simplification Advisory Group, U.S. House of Representatives

---

Transportation

Most transportation expenses are deductible except commuting expenses, home to your regular place of work and back, which are not deductible. See **Travel** and **Vehicles**.

Expense category: Car and truck expenses; or Travel (for overnight travel); or Other expenses.

Travel

Local business travel, when not going somewhere overnight, is limited to transportation expenses only. Regular commuting expenses, home to work and back, are not deductible. Side trips to customers or to suppliers are deductible.

You are allowed deductions for food and lodging and miscellaneous expenses only if you are away from home overnight. Home is defined as your place of business, not where you live. See **Food, Lodging**.

Self-employed itinerant workers, traveling contractors, and salespeople who are continually on the road are often denied travel deductions, the IRS claiming that the road is home, so nothing allowed.

If you are working away from home for over one year, the IRS automatically considers the road to be home, and disallows travel expenses.

Business Trips Within the U.S.

A business trip within the United States that is 100% business is 100% deductible. That includes round trip travel, lodging, transportation, and incidental expenses such as telephone, fax, laundry, etc. Two exceptions: Meals and entertainment are only 50% deductible. Deductions for travel on luxury boats or cruise ships have some limitations (check with the IRS).

Business Trips Outside the U.S.

A business trip outside the United States may also be 100% deductible (with the same exceptions of meals, entertainment and luxury water travel). But if you attend overseas conventions, seminars or meetings, a deduction is allowed only if the meeting is directly related to your business and if, in the IRS's opinion, there is a valid business reason for holding the meeting overseas. (Some countries are exempt from this restriction; check with the IRS.)

Business and Vacation Combined

What about a trip that is part business and part vacation? You may be able to deduct some of it, and you may be able to deduct all of it, if you carefully follow the rules.

If the reason for your trip is primarily personal (more than half the days are for vacation), none of the traveling expenses to and from your destination are deductible. Only expenses directly related to your business can be deducted.

If your trip is primarily for business (more than half the days are for business) and it is within the United States, the cost of the round-trip travel is fully deductible even if some of the trip is for pleasure. So you *can* tack a short vacation onto a business trip, and the only costs that aren't deductible are the non-business expenses, such as the extra days' lodging and meals and entertainment.

If you have a business trip that overlaps a weekend, requiring you to be there Friday and the following Monday, lucky you: you can write off the weekend as well, as a business expense, even though all you did was sit on the beach and dance in the clubs (as long as it is less expensive to stay the weekend than to go home Friday and come back Monday morning).

If you travel outside the U.S., more stringent rules apply. If the trip is no more than one week *or* the time spent for pleasure is less than 25 percent, the same basic rules apply as a trip within the U.S. But if the trip is more than a week, or if the vacation days are 25% or more of the trip, you must allocate travel expenses between the business and the personal portion of your trip.

When counting business versus vacation days, a "business day" does not require you to do business all day. Any day you put in at least four hours of work is considered a business day. Any day your presence is required, for any amount of time, is also considered a business day. And travel days also count as business days.

Deductible Expenses

Travel expenses typically include cost of transportation for you and your luggage to and from your destination; lodging and 50% of the cost of meals including tips (must not be "lavish or extravagant"); cost of transportation while away from home (taxi fares, auto rentals, etc.); entertainment, subject to the 50% limit; incidental expenses such as phone and fax; personal services (laundry, barbering, etc.).

Keeping Track of Expenses

For meals, lodging and incidental expenses, you can keep a record of actual expenses or, for some businesses, you can use a standard "per diem" rate set by the IRS—so much per day. See **Per Diem** and **Standard Meal Allowance** for more information.

Spouse, Family, Friend, Etc.

Travel expenses are not deductible for your spouse, dependent, friend, or anyone else, unless he or she is an employee or co-owner of the business, and there is a bona fide business purpose for accompanying you. This is a fairly new law. Husbands and wives used to be able to accompany their wives and husbands. This law was pushed through by a congressman who travels all over the world on a luxury military jet at taxpayer expense.

You can still deduct what it would cost you to travel alone. When deducting lodging, for example, you can write off the single-room rate at the hotel, which is often the same or slightly less than the double-room rate your family will actually pay.

The IRS Does Not Like Business Trips

As you can tell from the generous way the law is written, it's a bit too easy to write off a business trip that is really a disguised vacation. The IRS knows this all too well, and they are forever suspicious of business travel expenses, particularly sole proprietorships where the owner is accountable to no one else: you feel like taking a business trip (and you can afford it), you take it. The IRS wants to be sure it's not a vacation in disguise. You want to be sure you can prove, if audited, that the trip wasn't a vacation. A log of daily activities and business contacts is not required by law, but it may help convince a skeptical IRS auditor that your trip to the Bahamas or to New Orleans really was for business.

One tax client of mine who owned a retail coffee shop took an expensive trip to Scandinavia and wrote it off as a business deduction. When she was audited, which didn't surprise either of us, she was able to show the IRS auditor photos she took of coffee shops she visited throughout her travels. She showed the auditor Scandinavian coffee mugs that she is now importing. She got through the audit successfully.

For more information see IRS Publication 463, "Travel, Entertainment, and Gift Expenses." For per-diem rates and details, see IRS Publication 1542, "Per Diem Rates."

Expense category: Travel.

The point to remember is that what the government gives it must first take away.
                                                    —John S. Coleman

Trips, Business

Most business trips are deductible. See **Travel**.
Expense category: Travel.

Trucks

Trucks used for business can be deducted or depreciated like other vehicles. Vehicles have special limitations. See **Vehicles**.

Expense category: The category "Car and truck expenses" is for all vehicle expenses except the cost of the vehicle itself, which is deducted or depreciated under "Depreciation" (you must also fill out Form 4562, "Depreciation and Amortization").

Tuition

Some tuition is deductible. See **Education Expenses**.

Uncashed Checks

Are uncashed checks deductible? The answer depends on several factors: (1) Were the checks ever cashed? (2) Were they cashed in a different year than written? (3) Were the checks for large amounts of money? (4) Are you using the cash method or the accrual method of accounting?

Too many issues, too complicated. These tax laws are miserable. Let's start over.

Are uncashed checks deductible? An uncashed check was not really paid, was it? So it really isn't deductible. But most people take the deduction anyway and figure the check will get cashed sooner or later. A check written *and* mailed (or delivered) by December 31 can be written off the year it was written, even though it was not cashed until the new year.

Uncollectible Accounts

Uncollectible accounts are deductible as bad debts, but only if they were included in your income when you made the sale. Businesses using the cash method of accounting (recording income when the money comes in, not when the sale was made) cannot take a deduction for uncollectible accounts, because the income was not recorded in the first place. See **Bad Debts.**

Expense category: Bad debts.

The single most striking change in American life during the past twenty years is the redistribution of income from the working and middle class to the rich. It is not an act of God or even the inevitable workings of capitalism. It is caused by deliberate government tax policies.

—Molly Ivins, Fort Worth Star Telegram

"Under The Table" Payments

Did you actually look this item up, or just stumble upon it?

This interesting term, "under the table," means that a payment has been made, secretly, in cash, and no record is made of the payment. Under the table payments are sometimes made (so I'm told) to workers who are not officially on the payroll, to avoid payroll taxes and workers compensation insurance premiums, which is illegal and very risky and not a good idea at all.

But is an under-the-table payment deductible? If the payment was illegal, no deduction is allowed. If the secret payment was for some other reason and was legal (stranger things have happened in the business world), it is deductible. But if you didn't record it, you might have a difficult time proving it was made—and explaining why it was made—to an IRS auditor.

The term "off the books" means the same thing as "under the table."

Expense category: Depends on what the expense was for.

Unemployment Insurance

Employers pay state and federal unemployment insurance for their employees. This tax is deductible.

Sole proprietors, partners in partnerships, and members (owners) of limited liability companies are not subject to federal unemployment insurance. If you are required to pay state unemployment insurance, it is deductible.

Expense category: Insurance.

I haven't paid taxes in years, one of the reasons I believe everyone should run a business.

—Shirley A., magazine publisher, New Jersey

Unemployment Taxes

Employer's unemployment taxes are deductible.

Expense category: Taxes and licenses.

Unsalable Goods

Unsalable goods can be deducted as part of cost-of-goods-sold. See **Inventory**.

Expense category: Cost of goods sold.

Uniforms

Uniforms used exclusively for work are deductible. This includes costumes and protective gear. Cost of cleaning is also deductible.

Clothing with your company's logo or advertising is considered a uniform, and therefore deductible.

Expense category: Supplies.

Unions

Dues and meetings are deductible.

Expense category: Other expenses.

If part of your union dues are for political lobbying, that portion of the dues is not deductible.

Use Tax

Businesses are not usually required to collect sales tax on out-of-state sales. But in most states, the buyer is supposed to pay sales tax on mail-order purchases from out-of-state vendors—not to the seller, but directly to the state where you, the buyer, reside (unless the purchases are for resale).

No, I'm not kidding. When you buy a computer or office supplies from an out of state company, your own state wants you to pay sales tax on the purchase. It is called a use tax.

On your sales tax return, you will find a line where you calculate the use tax you owe, and pay it along with the sales tax you collected from your customers.

Any inventory or parts purchased tax-free but later used for a purpose other than resale, such as personal use, are also subject to the use tax.

This use tax is deductible. Normally, sales tax (which the use tax really is) is added to the cost of the goods. But since the use tax is paid after the fact, most businesses deduct it as another business tax.

There is a federal excise tax on truckers called a Highway Use Tax. This is a completely different tax than the use tax described above. It also is deductible.

Expense category: Taxes and licenses.

People will do silly things to avoid taxes.

—J. C. Small, Tax Attorney,
Counsel to the Director, New Jersey Division of Taxation

Utilities

Utilities, including electricity, gas, heating fuel, water, sewer service, and garbage pick up, are deductible.

Expense category: Utilities.

Home-Based Businesses: You can deduct a percentage of your home utilities only if you are allowed a home office deduction. See **Home Office**. Home-business utilities are deducted on Form 8829, "Expenses for Business Use of Your Home."

Manufacturers: Utilities for the manufacturing process may have to be added to the cost of the inventory rather than being written off immediately. See *Inventory*.

Vacation

Can you write off part of your vacation as a business expense? Yes, if it is combined with a legitimate business trip and if you follow the rules. See **Travel**.
Expense category: Travel.

The IRS sends out more than 250,000 incorrect collection bills each year to individuals who have paid up.
—General Accounting Office, U.S. Congress

Vacation Facilities

The IRS has restrictions on vacation facilities, especially when made available to employees. The Tax Courts, however, have ruled that vacation facilities for employees are fully deductible. If you own or lease a vacation facility, I suggest you talk to your accountant (who certainly will need to visit and examine the facility first hand to be sure it meets all IRS requirements).

Vacation Pay

An employer can deduct vacation pay for employees. The pay is treated as regular taxable wages.
Expense category: Wages.

How many honest politicians does it take to change a light bulb?
Both of them.

How many lobbyists does it take to change a light bulb?
None. But by offering an all-expense-paid trip to the Bahamas they can get a Congressman to do it.

How many farmers does it take to change a light bulb?
None. They get a tax subsidy for not changing them.

How many government employees does it take to change a light bulb?
45. One to change the bulb and 44 to handle the paperwork.

Vandalism

Deductible to the extent not covered by insurance.

Expense category: Depends on what kind of property was vandalized, and what costs are incurred.

Vans

Vans, busses, and transporters used for business can be deducted or depreciated like other vehicles. Vehicles have special limitations. See **Vehicles**.

Expense category: The category "Car and truck expenses" is for all vehicle expenses except the cost of the vehicle itself, which is deducted or depreciated under "Depreciation" (you must also file Form 4562, "Depreciation and Amortization").

Vehicles

All expenses of operating a vehicle for business are deductible except regular commuting expenses between your home and your usual place of business, which the IRS considers personal and not deductible. (Leased automobiles have certain limitations; see below).

There are two ways of figuring vehicle expenses.

Method One: You can keep itemized records of all your vehicle expenses. These include gasoline, oil, lubrication, maintenance, repairs, insurance, parking, tolls, garage rents, license and registration fees, even auto club dues. The purchase price of the vehicle and the cost of major repairs such as an engine overhaul may be deducted the year of purchase (with limitations) or depreciated over several years. See **Business Assets** and **Depreciation**.

Keeping itemized records of all your vehicle expenses is tedious work. The IRS realizes this also. In one of their rare helpful moods they have come up with Method Two, an optional Standard Mileage Allowance (Standard Mileage Rate):

Method Two: Instead of recording each fill up and every oil change, you may take a standard flat rate for every business mile driven (again, not including the commute). The rate per mile allowed by the IRS changes from year to year. The 2002 rate is 36½¢ per mile. This mileage allowance is in lieu of depreciation and all vehicle expenses except parking, tolls, interest, and state and local taxes, which are deductible in addition to the mileage allowance (sales tax on the vehicle is not deductible).

Vehicle expenses must be prorated between personal use (not deductible—and remember commuting to and from the office is considered personal use), and business use (fully deductible). The most common method of proration is based on the miles driven. For example, if you drove 10,000 miles last year of which 2,500 miles was for business, 25% of all your vehicle expenses are deductible, and 25% of the cost of your vehicle can be deducted or depreciated.

Some Fine Print: You may not use the Standard Mileage Allowance if you use the vehicle for hire such as a taxi, or if your business operates more than one vehicle at a time (you can use more than one vehicle for business as long as both vehicles are not being used at the same time). Business vehicles that do not qualify for the Standard Mileage Allowance may still use Method One, itemizing expenses. Using the standard mileage rate reduces the cost basis of your vehicle (for figuring profit or loss when the vehicle is sold).

If you use the Standard Mileage Allowance, you must reduce the cost basis of your vehicle by 15¢ per mile, for every business mile driven, all years combined. The IRS says that 15¢ per mile is the "depreciation portion" of the allowance. When you sell the vehicle, the reduced cost basis will affect the profit or loss on the sale.

The method you choose the first year you use your vehicle for business determines what methods you can use in future years (for that vehicle). If you use Method One (itemizing) the first year, you must stay with that method as long as you use that vehicle. If you use Method Two (the Standard Mileage Allowance) the first year, you can switch back and forth if you want, itemizing some years and using the mileage allowance other years. If you do switch from the mileage allowance to itemizing, you must use straight line depreciation.

Depreciation and first year write off on a vehicle is limited if the vehicle costs over a certain amount.

You should check with your accountant to find out the most advantageous way to write off your vehicle.

Whichever method you choose, keep a log of the business miles driven. If you estimate your miles, you're likely to cheat yourself. You can put 25 miles on your car just running errands around town.

Expense category: "Car and truck expenses" is for all vehicle expenses except the cost of the vehicle itself, which is deducted or depreciated under "Depreciation" (and you must also fill out Form 4562, "Depreciation and Amortization").

Leasing and rentals: Automobile leases, if 30 days or longer, are not 100% deductible. The IRS has a table, called "Inclusion Amounts for Cars," that shows how much of an auto lease can and cannot be deducted. See IRS Publication 463 for the table. This rules does not apply to trucks, vans or heavy sport utility vehicles, which are fully deductible.

For more information, see IRS Publ. 917, "Business Use of a Car" and IRS Publ. 463, "Travel, Entertainment, Gift and Car Expenses."

It's getting harder and harder to support the government in the style to which it has become accustomed.   —*Farmer's Almanac*

Voided Checks

It must be pretty obvious that you do not get a deduction for a voided check you wrote and then tore up. If you don't void the check immediately, and you've already taken a deduction for it, reverse the deduction out of your ledgers.

Every bill has the force of police power behind it. Every bill changes the method of how laws are enforced. And yet, legislators usually do not read all of the legislation they vote on, and they consistently vote on legislation without understanding what it is. On one occasion late in a session, when things were all jammed up, we had a great number of bills on the consent calendar. In one fell swoop, we voted on 25 bills at one time.
—Former California Senator H.R. Richardson

Wages

Employee wages are deductible. See **Payroll**.
Expense category: Wages.

If your business is not a corporation, your own wages—that is, the wages you pay yourself if you pay yourself a wage—are not a deductible business expense. See **Draw** and **Paying Yourself**.

Warehouse

The cost of renting a warehouse is deductible. The cost of a building (or part of a building) you own can be depreciated. See **Buildings**. The cost of warehouse space in your home is deductible only if you meet certain home office requirements. See **Home Office**.
Expense category: Rent or lease (for rented space); Depreciation (owned building); Form 8829, "Expenses for Business Use of Your Home" (for home based businesses).

Watch Dog

The cost of buying, feeding and maintaining a watch dog is

deductible. The animal itself may have to be depreciated over its expected life.

Expense category: Other expenses. Depreciation.

The apparent acquiescence of the American people in governmental extravagance induced a prodigality in the disposition of public funds which has gone on unabated to the present day. —Mr. F.C. Howe, 1896

Water

Water and other utilities are deductible.
Expense category: Utilities.

Home-Based Businesses: You can deduct a percentage of your home utilities only if you are allowed a home office deduction. See **Home Office.** Home-business utilities are deducted on Form 8829, "Expenses for Business Use of Your Home."

Manufacturers: Water for the manufacturing process may have to be added to the cost of the inventory rather than being written off immediately. See **Inventory.**

Web Page or Web Site

The cost of designing and setting up a Web page is deductible. If the amount is significant, it may have to be amortized (depreciated) over three years. See **Depreciation.**

Hosting fees and costs of maintaining a Web site are deductible.

The cost of Internet access is fully deductible if used only for business. If used partly for non business, you must prorate the cost and deduct only the business portion.

Expense category: Advertising (Web page); Depreciation (expensive web site); Office expense (access, hosting, etc.).

Wife on Payroll

See **Spouse.**

Compiled from reports in the New York Times, the Washington Post, the Wall Street Journal, and the Baltimore Sun:

In the final days of the last session, members of Congress spent $102,000 of taxpayers' money filling 248 pages of the Congressional Record with praise for retiring and defeated lawmakers.

The Congressional restaurants print new menus every day at a cost of $100,000 a year.

The Pentagon leases computers for $1 billion a year that it could have purchased for $200,000.

Five private dining rooms at the Pentagon reserved for military brass provide cut-rate meals ($2.65 for a steak) at a cost to taxpayers of $1.3 million a year.

At least 175 federal employees in Washington are driven to and from work in chauffeured government-owned vehicles at a cost of $4.8 million a year.

The U.S. Office of Smallpox Eradication has an annual budget of $1.2 million. Smallpox was eradicated on earth many years ago.

A few years ago, Congress spent $3 million to automate elevators on Capitol Hill. Most of the elevators still have operators, 89 in all, at an annual cost of $890,000.

The Air National Guard spent $110,000 to fly 431 officers from twelve cities to a bowling tournament in Nashville.

The Franklin Delano Roosevelt Memorial Commission, a government agency created in 1955 to devise a plan for a monument to F.D.R., spent $40,000 a year, for 42 years, before finally designing and building the monument, which opened in 1997. In 1998, the Commission reconvened to start revisions to the monument.

The Internal Revenue Service

Work Clothes

Deductible only if unsuitable for street wear (but see **Uniforms**). Cost of cleaning work clothes is deductible.

Clothing with your company's logo or advertising is fully deductible, even though the clothing may be suitable for street wear.

Expense category: Supplies, or Advertising.

Work In Process

Work in process (also called work in progress) is a manufacturing term for a product that is partially completed. Work in process is part of your inventory and cannot be deducted until sold. See **Inventory**.

Expense category: Cost of goods sold.

Workshop

The cost of renting a workshop is deductible. The cost of a building you own can be depreciated. See **Buildings**. The cost of a home-based workshop is deductible only if you meet the home office requirements. See **Home Office**.

Expense category: Rent or lease (for rented space); Depreciation (owned building); Form 8829, "Expenses for Business Use of Your Home" (for home based businesses).

Workers' Compensation Insurance

Workers' compensation insurance an employer pays to cover employees is deductible.

Workers' compensation insurance you pay for yourself is deductible only if your state requires you to have workers comp insurance on yourself. If the coverage is voluntary, the premiums are not deductible (except for corporations).

Expense category: Insurance.

It is our Patriotic Duty to keep as much money out of the hands of our government as we can. —Philosopher Walter Camp

---

Worthless Goods

Worthless inventory can be written off as part of cost of goods sold. See **Inventory**.

Worthless business assets that have already been fully deducted cannot be deducted a second time. If the assets are being depreciated, the remaining undepreciated balance can be deducted. For example, let's say you bought a piece of equipment a few years ago for $4,000, and you've already taken $2,500 depreciation on it. It dies and isn't worth fixing. Since you've already deducted $2,500, you can only deduct $1,500, which is the undepreciated balance.

Expense category: Depreciation. You must also fill out Form 4562, "Depreciation and Amortization."

See, Jimmy? If they give a big tax cut to the wealthy, those guys'll feel good and have us come fix their roof and stuff.

Yellow Pages

Yellow Pages listings and advertising are deductible.
Expense category: Advertising.

Zoning

Costs of zoning permits, filings, hearings, appeals, petitions, etc. are deductible.
Expense category: Taxes and licenses.

Small business is where we have the most trouble.
—IRS Commissioner Charles O. Rossotti

Keeping Current

Tax laws change every year. *422 Tax Deductions* is revised and updated every printing. If you are reading an older edition of this book, be careful to verify any information to be sure it is still current.

Annual Update Sheet

Every January we publish a one-page Tax Update. If you would like a copy of the Update, send a self-addressed, stamped #10 envelope (business size) and $1.00 to: 422 Update, Box 1240, Willits, CA 95490.

New Edition Offer

We offer a 25% discount off the purchase price of a new edition if you turn in the title page of any earlier edition.

E-Mail Newsletter

If you would like to receive our free e-mail newsletter, which includes update information for all of our books, send your e-mail address to newsletter@bellsprings.com. Subscribers to our newsletter will not be put on any mail lists; we do not give our customers' names to anyone.

Questions?

If you have any questions, suggestions, or comments about *422 Tax Deductions*, please send them to Bernard Kamoroff, c/o Bell Springs Publishing, PO Box 1240, Willits, California 95490. Or e-mail Kamoroff@bellsprings.com.

Quality Small Business Books & Software from Bell Springs Publishing

27th Edition:
Small Time Operator:
How to Start Your Own Business, Keep Your Books, Pay Your Taxes & Stay Out of Trouble
Bernard Kamoroff, C.P.A.

Be Your Own Boss. Here is the help you need to take control of your life and be a success, on your own terms. For all businesses and self-employed individuals, here—in an all-new, fully revised and expanded edition—is complete, up-to-date information:

Getting all your permits & licenses. How to finance your business. Finding the right business location. Creating & using a business plan. Choosing & protecting your business name. How to set up a complete yet simple bookkeeping system. Do you need to incorporate? Hiring employees. Buying a business or franchise. Federal, state & local taxes. Internet businesses. Dealing with—and avoiding!—the IRS. Insurance, contracts, pricing, trademarks...and much more.
With 600,000 copies in print, *Small Time Operator* has sold more copies than any other business start-up guide ever published.

#02   224 pages, paperback, 8½"x11"   **$17.95**

Online Operator:
Business, Legal and Tax Guide to the Internet
Bernard Kamoroff, C.P.A.

Stake your claim on the Internet, and avoid costly legal trouble along the way. For both new and ongoing businesses, and all self-employed individuals and professionals, here is complete, up-to-date coverage of the legal, tax, and nuts-and-bolts business issues for Web sites, e-commerce, and survival on the Internet.

- Setting up an Internet business: legal structure, permits, licenses, financing, insurance, bookkeeping.
- The "tax free" Internet: tax laws and federal regulations.
- Web sites: design, hosting, secure servers, online ordering, credit cards, technical and legal issues.
- Trademarks and domain names.
- Online copyrights and patents.
- Licensing, privacy, security, and liability issues.
- Fraud, theft, and hacker protection.
- International laws, exporting, and overseas sales.
- Home-based Internet businesses.
- *And much more.*

#03   240 pages, paperback, 7"x9"   **$18.95**

Marketing Without Advertising
Michael Phillips & Salli Rasberry

Does advertising work? Do you need to advertise? Are there better ways to market your business?

The first part of this startling book argues convincingly and with documented proof that almost all advertising is totally ineffective and an utter waste of money; and that most business owners have been successfully duped into believing that advertising is both necessary and productive in spite of obvious evidence to the contrary.

Marketing Without Advertising is much more than an argument against advertising. Packed into this little gem of a book are more than a hundred tried and tested marketing strategies that have worked for all kinds of small businesses. Here is what you need to know to successfully promote your business—at little or no cost.

Possibly the last $19 you'll ever spend on advertising!

#04   185 pages, 7"x9", paperback   **$18.95**

Free Help From Uncle Sam
To Start or Expand Your Business
William Alarid & Gustav Berle

Here, in one convenient source, are several hundred government programs and agencies that purchase from small businesses and that offer services, publications and financial assistance to small businesses:

Government loan programs and financial incentives. Import and export assistance. Census information and statistics. Special programs for women, minorities and handicapped people. Free small business information and counseling. State by state listings for Federal Information Centers, SBA field offices, International Trade Administration offices, Small Business Development Centers, and each state's Small Business Assistance program and offices.

Includes a list of government agencies that purchase from small businesses, and explains how you can sell your goods and services to these agencies.

#05   233 pages, 5½"x8½"   **$17.95**

Basic Guide to
Selling Arts & Crafts
James Dillehay

Artists and craftspeople can fine tune their business, and novices can learn how to turn a hobby into a livelihood: Product lines. Wholesaling. Consignment. Displays. Shows. Pricing. Discounts. Dealing with show promoters, sales reps, store and gallery owners. Finding sales outlets. Licensing. And more.

This is the Official Training Guide used by the American Crafters Guild and the Association of Creative Crafts. The author is on the Advisory Board of the National Craft Association.

#06   220 pages, 6"x9", paperback   **$14.95**

Small Time Operator: The Software
Bernard Kamoroff CPA, Steve Steinke & Emil Krause

For people with a spreadsheet program, here is the same bookkeeping system as the one in *Small Time Operator*, on a ready-to-use spreadsheet file (template). The disk contains 23 spreadsheets: Income and Expenditure ledgers. Profit and loss statement. Balance Sheet. Payroll. Cash Flow. Net worth. Petty cash. Partners' capital. Credit ledger. Inventory control. Business plan. Invoice form. Mailing list. Loan amortization. Telephone-address file. Includes 184-page manual.

    This is not a stand-alone program. You *must* have Lotus 1-2-3, Quattro Pro, Excel, or Works spreadsheet program. (PC only. Not available on Macintosh.)
#07   184 page manual & disk.   **$29.95**

We Own It:
Starting & Managing Cooperatives and Employee Owned Businesses
Peter Honigsberg, Attorney at Law & Bernard Kamoroff, C.P.A.

The only book of its kind, *We Own It* gives you the legal, tax and management information you need to start and operate all types of consumer, producer and worker co-ops. Covers non-profit, for-profit and cooperative corporations, ESOP's, and all other options.
#08   150 pages, 8½"x11", paperback   **$14.00**

Getting Into The Mail Order Business
Julian L. Simon

Everything you need to know to get started and be a success in mail order:
   The kinds of products that naturally sell well in mail order, and those that don't. How to locate and test your market and promote your products. Selling through catalogs. How *not* to compete with the large mail order houses. How to create mail order copy that works.
   And more: Setting up shop. Where to go for direct mail lists. Handling shipping, refunds, guarantees. How the mail order laws affect your business.
#09   291 pages, 6"x9", paperback   **$14.95**

Negotiating the Purchase or Sale of a Business
James C. Comiskey

This thorough guide will help a buyer determine if a business is worth buying. How profitable the business presently is. How good are the location and the lease. How easy or hard will it be for a new owner to take over. How much to expect to pay. How to value the inventory and assets. How much to pay for "goodwill".
   This guide will help the seller determine a fair asking price, prepare for the sale, and deal with prospective buyers. Includes legal and tax aspects of a sale, the contract, & common financing arrangements.
#10   137 pgs., 40 worksheets, 8½"x11", paper   **$18.95**

Starting Young
Joe Mellin

Sixteen year old Joe Mellin is not only a great business-kid (he started and successfully operated three after-school businesses), he's an excellent writer as well, explaining in this concise guide how any kid with an idea and a little go get 'em can start your own business, have fun, and earn real money. Forget begging your parents for an allowance, get this book and live life like a king.
#11   108 pages, 6"x9"   **$12.00**

Selling To Uncle Sam
C.L. Crownover & M. Henricks

Find out how you can join the many businesses successfully selling to our government, how to get your company on the government's select bid list, how to maneuver through the rules and red tape. It's work, but it's worth it!
#12   205 pages, 6"x9", hardback   **$17.95**

Marketing Myths
K.J. Clancy & R.S. Shulman

Marketing—spreading the word about your product or service—is essential to *every* business, big or small. Here is the help you need to cut through the theories and myths, and deal with the real world of finding and keeping customers and clients.
#13   309 pages, 6"x9", hardback   **$19.95**

The Entrepreneurial PC
Bernard J. David

A hundred businesses you can start using word processing, desktop publishing, online information research, database marketing, e-mail, computer graphics, and accounting, bookkeeping and payroll programs.
#14   294 pages, 7"x9", paperback   **$17.95**

Legal Help for Your Business
Mead Hedglon

Save both your money and your sanity in dealing with legal matters: when you don't need lawyers, how to avoid litigation, and if necessary, how to get the best help at the lowest possible cost.
#15   296 pages, 6"x9", hardback   **$16.95**

Golden Entrepreneuring
James B. Arkebauer

A "golden" wealth of tips and ideas how to use your years and experience to your advantage. Real, hands-on help for those of you fed up with the corporate struggle or bored with retirement, and looking to have some fun—and make some money
#16   254 pages, 6"x9", paperback   **$16.95**